If you dream of being the hit of the party
or the bar, take some tips from
Ed McMahon

"Johnny Carson's 'HERE'S JOHNNY' man and
celebrated elbow-bender of Television Row chats
with his readers and offers his personal collection
of barside games, stunts, jokes and sleight-of-hand
tricks for killing a pleasant hour—or for laying
bets with a pal. Read cold, they're amusing; mem-
orized and performed with a few under the belt,
they can—in one sense or another—be devastating."

—*Publishers' Weekly*

ED McMAHON'S BARSIDE COMPANION
was originally published by
The World Publishing Company.

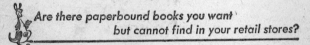

Ed McMahon's Barside Companion

Drawings by
Phil Interlandi

PUBLISHED BY POCKET BOOKS NEW YORK

ED McMAHON'S BARSIDE COMPANION

World Publishing edition published November, 1969

Pocket Book edition published October, 1970

This *Pocket Book* edition includes every word
contained in the original, higher-priced edition. It is printed
from brand-new plates made from completely reset, clear, easy-to-read
type. *Pocket Book* editions are published by Pocket Books, a division
of Simon & Schuster, Inc., 630 Fifth Avenue, New York, N.Y. 10020.
Trademarks registered in the United States and other countries.

Table of Contents

PART I

WHEN GOOD FRIENDS GET TOGETHER 1

Introduction 3

You Wanta Bet? *or* If There's One Born Every
Minute, What About That Guy On the Next Barstool? 7

Seeing is Believing 16

And With a Little Dexterity 21

Geometricks 30

Games (Drinking) People Play *or* Breaking the Ice
Is More Fun Than Watching It Melt 40

What's The Good Word *or* Scrambled Sayings,
Swifties, Hink Dinks and Beyond 62

The Numbers Games *or* How to Add and Subtract
Your Way To Success 71

Ah, Sweet Mysteries of Life *or* So You Want to be
a Detective 82

Let's Have a Psych-in *or* The Doctor Is In 88

Magic Made Easy *or* Sleight Hand For Every Man 97

PART II

THE GENTLEMANLY ART OF DRINKING 113

A Few Kind Words About Man's
Second Favorite Pastime 117

History of Alcohol or More Than You Need To
Know About How It all Started 121

Drinking in America or Documents of (Happily)
Yesteryear 131

The Drinking Man or .003 Isn't Much, But It's A
Start 143

W. C. Fields or The Drinking Man's Drinking Man 151

Definitions for the Drinking Man or Words to Wet
Your Whistle By 154

The Ultimate Weapon or An Itsy, Bitsy, Teeny,
Weeny Extra Special Dry Martini 162

The Curse of the Drinking Man or The Care,
Treatment and Cause of The American Hangover 166

The Loaded Sobriety Test or How To Send Them
Home Filled with Confidence (Among Other
Things) 171

Drinking for Profit or They Said It Couldn't Be
Done And It Can't 175

Gentlemen, Charge Your Glasses! 177

Surely It Can't Be Closing Time! 178

WHEN GOOD FRIENDS
GET
TOGETHER

Introduction

Hi. I'm Ed McMahon. I see we're cleaning olives off toothpicks by the same dim light. Come here often? Like it? I can't think of a better place to pass the time a man spends waiting to meet his wife. You met Bill? A great bartender. I've known him for years. He used to say his customers were here for one of two reasons: either they didn't have a wife to go home to—or they did.

My wife complains now and then about my talking to strangers in bars. And I tell her, "Honey, there *are* no strangers in bars." Maybe she's worried about those secretaries I hear telling Bill how their bosses' wives don't understand them. Those kind of problems I'll leave to Bill and you young fellas.

But there's another problem I have learned to solve: you might call it what to do while the ice melts. Over the years I've collected some simple games you can play in a bar—or, for that matter, any place people gather for a little easygoing conviviality. Want me to tell you about them? It'll help us pass an hour or two. And, if you pay attention to your Uncle Ed, you can learn a lot.

3

Some of them are games to give you something to do while they're televising one of those half-time gabfests during the football games. I know some others which will win you a lot of drinks, but I wouldn't try them on a guy who might be a member of the vice squad. I've also got some story games which require only a little dexterity of the mental kind.

And then there are numbers games. Would you believe I've got one you could use to get that blonde to tell you how old she is, and how many times she's been engaged?

You can play psych-ins—games where you can find out what makes other people tick, whether they want to let you wind their mainspring or not. And I've got a raft of betchas (you know, "I betcha I can." or "I betcha you can't . . ."). Loaded? You bet! I've got a shell game a 10-year-old can work, if you're fool enough to show him how. And there's one that's as simple as challenging some-one to find out where the numeral 1776 appears on a dollar bill. Go ahead. Look now . . . Find it?

Then I've got some slightly sleight-of-hand tricks I'll tell you about. How'd you like to be able to leave a tip on the bar for a surly bartender—under an upside-down glass filled with beer? I'll show you how.

You've heard of fireside companions—well, put togeth-er, all this gamesmanship, trickery, knavery, numerology and sleightery turns out to be something of a barside companion. Not that some of this lore can't be put to good use around your own rumpus room. I've got a McMahon sobriety test to give your guests before you send them home—and believe me, you'll send them home reeling, even if they're sober.

It's all in good fun. The point is that even if you blow a trick or lose a game, you've accomplished your main pur-pose: to break the ice, to make the hours flow more pleas-antly, and—if you're lucky—to make a friend.

But there's another side to this barside companion. It's

all about what we've been doing plenty of. It's called "The Gentlemanly Art of Drinking" and contains jokes, limericks, toasts, hangover cures—as well as a great deal of fascinating historical information, from the text of the Eighteenth Amendment to the more lasting drinking laws of W. C. Fields. I think you'll find it interesting.

A word of thanks to Dial Torgerson and Abraham Hurwitz. Both gentlemen helped immeasurably in gathering the material and preparing the manuscript for this book.

Okay. Charge your glasses, ladies and gentlemen! And please begin.

You Wanta Bet?
or
If There's One Born Every Minute, What About That Guy On The Next Barstool?

There's an old gamblers' saying that if a guy bets you he can make the one-eyed jack jump out of the deck and squirt cider in your ear, don't take it—because you'll end up with an ear full of cider every time.

That's because when a guy offers you a bet on what looks like a sure thing, he's got something tricky up his sleeve. After all, why would he make the offer? Still, there really is one born every minute—and he (or she) just might be sitting at the next bar-stool.

At the cost of buying innumerable drinks for guys with bland, honest faces—and nimble tongues and limber fingers—I've been able to collect a few pages of sure things. Bet with me, my friend, and you'll never lose a double martini. I call them Betchas. You know, I betcha that . . . Try them out and see what luck you have.

The Ample Turnover

Three moves should be ample for you to turn these coins over two at a time so that they end up heads-tails, heads-tails, heads-tails:

Didn't do it? Then follow my simple instructions:
First turnover: 3 and 4
Second: 4 and 5
Lastly: 2 and 3.
And see what you've got?

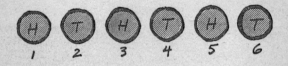

Bottoms Up

Let's arrange three glasses—to be original, we'll name them a, b and c—in this order:

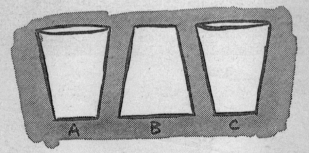

And what I want you to do is to turn them all bottoms up in three moves, turning over two glasses at a time.

Give up? Be my guest:

First, turn over glasses b and c.

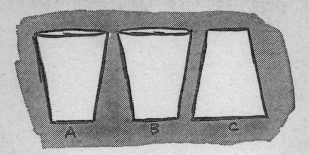

Second, turn over a and c.

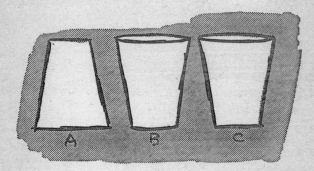

Lastly, turn over b and c.

There they are, bottoms up.

If you want to be really nasty about it, there's a way to foil your victim even after you've showed him how to do it. Simply start off with the glasses in this position:

as opposed to the way it was set up originally. Look closely. Each glass is reversed. In three moves he will wind up with all the bottoms down!

The Sneaky Splash

Comedians have what they call "groaners"—jokes so bad the audience groans at the punch line. There are groaners in the art of gamesmanship, too, and here's one of them:

Set out five glasses, two full of water, this way—

And then challenge the other fella to arrange them into alternately empty and full, by moving only one glass. The glasses should end up this way:

After the poor guy has spent 20 minutes maneuvering glasses up and down the bar, without success, tell him the answer: just empty 1 into 4.

You may well end up wearing the glass of water. Don't blame me. Didn't I tell you it was a groaner?

Floatation

Bet your friends in the neighborhood saloon you can make a needle float on a glass of water. But offer to let them try it first.

In case you've never tried it, needles just don't like to float. Not even when you settle them in water ever so gently.

When it's your turn to show how it's done, tear off a piece of paper napkin, float it on top of a glass of water, and then drop a dry needle on the piece of paper. The paper will absorb the water and sink out from under the needle. And the needle, thus delicately launched, will float.

By the way, if you want to make the trick even more impressive, magnetize one end of the needle first. Then it'll float with one end pointing north, and you can use it to find your way home after the sore losers kick you out of the bar.

Where do you get the magnet? Same place you got the needle, of course. You can find almost anything behind a bar—if you look long enough.

Sneaky Petes

You'll never lose a drink betting someone:

That he can't answer four questions wrong, no matter how hard he tries.

—Ask him three questions to which he gives you wrong answers. Then, pretending to lose track, ask, "Let me see—that's three questions so far, isn't it?" He'll undoubtedly say "yes," thus answering your fourth question correctly.

That he can't take off his coat alone.

—When he starts taking off his coat, you just take yours off, too.

That he can't answer this one.

The U.S. Constitution specifies four requirements for becoming President of the United States. He has to be at least 35, born a citizen, and must have lived in this country at least 14 years. What's the fourth?

—He has to be elected!

And here's one that'll never lose you a buck, although it certainly sounds like it will.

Bet someone $1 that if he gives you $2, you'll give him back $4.

—After he gives you the $2, you look thoughtful a moment, and then say, "Well, I guess I can't do it, after all."

Then you give him back one of the two dollars he gave you. After all, you lost the bet. But you keep the other dollar!

Now you know why they're called Sneaky Petes!

The Asbestos Dollar

Dollars burn. Everybody knows that. So this makes a pretty good betcha: bet you can't burn my dollar with your lighted cigarette.

Here's how you win this one: wrap the bill around a glass, holding it tight with your thumb and forefinger, this way:

The cigarette won't harm your dollar. Why? Because the glass absorbs the heat, keeping the paper below its ignition point.

The Unruly Pen

Take a business card and, drawing freehand, draw an X on the back. Then bet the lady next door a fresh martini she can't do it backward. Yours will look like this:

Chances are she'll think you mean just drawing the lines going in the opposite direction from the way you drew them. Then you explain that when you said backward, you meant it. She has to do it in a mirror. Borrow the mirror from her purse. Put it up against a glass, and put the card in front of it, and ask her to draw the same X without looking at the card—only at the mirror. It'll come out like this:

For some reason, it's impossible to draw straight lines backward, using a mirror. She'll miss the corners every time.

Strike Out

You've heard of people making bets about whether or

not a cigarette lighter will work the first time? I advise against getting mixed up in this hot controversy. Try a little counterpunching instead. When some guy is bragging about how well his lighter works, bet him he can't even light all the matches in a book of matches, striking each one only one time.

Use a little reverse psychology. Hint that the reason it's hard to do is there's too much pressure for the average man to strike with accuracy. ("I'm not saying that an astronaut couldn't do it. But for just an average guy . . .")

But here's the secret, my friend. It's a matter of sulfur, not self assurance. There's sulfur on the striking surface, see? And toward the end of the book of matches it begins to get used up, making a second swipe necessary.

Be nice when the other guy fails. Tell him something like, "Yeah, I know. It's tough to come through when the screws are really on you." You're not supposed to give away the secret, you know. Unless you notice he looks a bit like he's going to cry and you find out that he IS an astronaut.

Seeing is Believing

Here are some betchas that test one's powers of observation. My friend Al, who is in computers, wears tweeds and smokes a pipe, uses them to break even when he's stuck next to one of those bright young men at a party or a friendly local hostelry. They simply prove that none of us is as smart—observant, actually—as we think we are.

Bigger Round The Top

You point to a fellow's beer glass, one of those tall, slim pilsners, and say: "I bet your glass is bigger around the top than it is tall." How will he be able to resist a bet like that? "You're on," he'll say.

Then you measure. A piece of string works fine, but you can use a paper napkin. Or, if there's a Southern Congressman in the bar, borrow his string tie. Measure the circumference around the top, then the height of the part of the glass that holds the beer.

The circumference, surprisingly enough, will be greater, every time.

You Never Know

The brighter people are, the more it hurts them to be confounded by trivia—including questions like these:

How many keys are there on the standard typewriter? Come within one of the right answer.

—42 or 43. That's why we gave you the leeway.

Besides "Coin return," what other word appears on the coin-return box of a pay telephone?

—Pull Down.

Is Lincoln wearing a tie on the penny? Is Jefferson, on the nickel?

—Lincoln yes, Jefferson no.

What letter doesn't appear on the telephone dial?

—Ever hear of a "Q" prefix?

Which is at the top of the traffic signal, the red light or the green one?

—Red.

Hey, Look Me Over!

Give a friend 15 seconds to find on a dollar bill—

1. Four eyes.

(Washington has two. The third is on top of the pyramid on the back side of the bill. And the eagle shows us a fourth.)

2. A scale.

(On the front of the bill, to the right of Washington's picture, is a green circle, the seal. In the center of it is a scale.)

3. A key.

(It's in the same green circle to the right of Washington.)

4. The number 1776.

(It's in Roman numerals at the base of the pyramid.)

5. At least twenty ones.

(You may have to include some from the serial numbers—and the Roman numeral.)

We know now, even if we didn't before, that George Washington is on the dollar bill. (Remember, we counted his eyes?) But what about the faces on the other bills?

Most people know who's on the five (Lincoln) and the ten (Alexander Hamilton). But what about the ones that are harder to remember? Give a friend 15 seconds to tell us whose picture is on the:

—Two dollar bill (Thomas Jefferson)

—Twenty (Andrew Jackson)

—Fifty (U.S. Grant)

—Hundred (Benjamin Franklin)

Take Another Look

Observant, are you? Then read this sentence:

My ability to fool folks magically is the result of years of scientific study combined with the experience of years.

All I ask is this: Count the Fs in the sentence. Only once! Don't go back.

The average person finds 3, above average 4, and a superior observer sees 5. There are actually 6. Go ahead! Count them again!

Double Your Money

Place a coin in the center of a table plate in which you have previously placed some water. Next, take a drinking glass and cover the coin. When seen from above, through the glass, it looks as if there are two coins there instead of one. (This is caused by light passing through the water.)

Bet a friend to guess how many coins there are in the plate—and, if he says two, you'll collect.

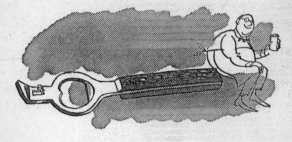

Just A Minute Now!

Next time someone excuses himself (or herself) from your table "for a minute," ask those left behind to tell you how long a minute is. I'm serious. It's amazing how hard it is for people to accurately guess a minute—even by counting. And if you have at least two people competing and the one who is farthest off has to buy the next round, you'd be surprised the pressure it puts on them. Usually they underguess. When you're doing nothing but waiting for it to pass, a minute seems like a long, long time.

19

Of course, if that someone who was excused from your table was a woman, intent on something like "fixing her face," you'll need more than the help of a second hand for measuring her minute.

And With a Little
Dexterity

Some betchas take a little nimbleness of finger or quickness of hand. These are the kind where you have to do something to win a bet. I remember one this old carnival con artist used to pull in a little bar down on Third Avenue. "Put a shot of whiskey under my hat," he'd say, "and I'll show you how I can empty it without touching the hat."

Some fool would buy a shot of whiskey and the old sharpy would put his hat over it, and then lean over the hat, concentrating hard and sniffing deeply as though he were somehow absorbing the whiskey by some kind of osmosis. Then he'd suddenly announce, triumphantly, "There!"

The guy who bought the drink would snatch the hat up to see what had happened. He'd been taken, that's what had happened. Because the old con man would grab that shot of whiskey and drink it down—glug! Just as he said. Without touching his hat.

His particular dexterity was in guzzling the drink before his donor realized what was going on. Some of these others take a bit more skill. You might practice them once or twice before you tell someone you'll do the impossible or else buy drinks for the house. Most are pretty easy. Doing the impossible is all in knowing how.

The Shell Game

That same old carny hand tried to explain to me how the pros work the old shell game, where there's a pea under one of three walnut halves. You never know where it is and they always do. They do it by remembering some little distinguishing mark on the key shell, and then keeping track of it by some kind of mental gymnastics no matter how many times the shells are moved around.

The oldtimer showed me a simpler verson he said any fool could play (you see what he thought of my abilities). You turn three cups over on the bar and let the other player put a sugar cube under one of them, betting him you can pick out the right cup, even if you aren't looking when he hides the cube. And you can, too.

What you do is take a pinch of salt and sprinkle a few grains around the rim of each cup, without the other fellow noticing it, before he hides the sugar cube. Then you warn him he has to clean out the inside of the chosen cup with a napkin, first—"to remove psychic static," or something like that. In doing so he'll dislodge the grains of salt. After he puts the cube under that cup, no matter how much he shifts the three around, a few grains of salt will remain on the cups which don't have the sugar cube beneath them.

So it's a cinch for you to hum a few bars of "Lydia, dear Lydia, Lydia the Queen of Tattoo," and turn over the cup which has the cube beneath it.

The Salted Cellar

Here's another trick worth its salt:

While you're alone at the bar, heap up a big pile of salt, and then firmly balance a salt shaker in it at a 45-degree angle. Then carefully blow away most of the salt, leaving just a minimum of salt for support.

When your friends return, challenge them to duplicate it. They'll try to balance the salt shaker on the tiny bit of salt left. It can't be done.

Falling Buck

"Here's a crisp new dollar bill which I am going to hold between your thumb and forefinger," you say to a new friend or an old buddy. "I bet you can't catch it when I let it go! You think you can? Okay, let's try . . ."

What happens? It falls so fast that he can't catch it. He may try again and again, but the chances are the dollar bill will still slip through his fingers. Then he will probably challenge you to do it (for the next round?). You accept the challenge . . . and you catch it before it hits the floor!

How? By a little flim-flam . . .

When he has thumb and forefinger at the ready, you hold the buck so his fingers are in the middle of the bill. Almost no one can move fast enough to catch half a bill.

When you do it, move your fingers down toward the bottom of the bill. You will then have about two-thirds of it to catch. That makes a lot of difference. With a little practice, you can catch it almost every time.

Of course, after a few complimentary rounds, the really nice guy will reveal how it's done. And you really are a nice guy, aren't you?

23

Catch No. 2

There's a double catch in this one. The first is easy. Ahh, but the second one . . .

Hold a glass and, with your fingertips, a pair of dice, one on top of the other.

Now ask your friend to do the same, and then toss the dice one at a time into the glass.

They'll try again and again, without success. What makes it hard is the fact that to throw the second die into the air high enough to catch it with the glass also throws die No. 1 out of the glass.

After the losers have agreed to buy you a magnum of champagne if you can do it, do it:

The trick is to not toss the second one in the air, but to drop it—and then quickly drop the glass under the falling die, catching it before it hits the floor. Cling! You've done it: catch No. 2.

Snap!

Balance two pennies on the edge of a water glass. Here's the challenge: remove both at the same moment with only two fingers.

Here's how:

1. Snap them down flat on the glass, like this—

2. Move them down to the middle of the glass—

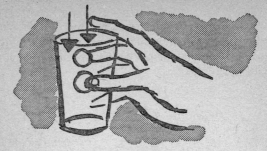

3. Pull them off, snapping them together.

(If you can't do it the first time, neither could I. Try again.)

Knotty Problem

The challenge here: tie a simple square knot in a length of string without letting go of the ends. (Where to get the string? I ask Bill, the bartender, for my string, but a good-sized handkerchief will do if you don't know your guy that well.)

When people try and fail, tell them they have to start by folding their arms. The contortions which follow will be great to film for a home movie. It's easy when you know exactly how:

1. When you pick up the rope, do so after you've crossed your arms, with the right hand under the left armpit, and your left hand twisted over the top of your right elbow, like this:

2. Then simply pull your arms apart, and the rope will form a knot as you do so.

The Splash Platform

Give your friends this much equipment:

Then ask them to arrange the empty glasses in such a way that the knives will support the glass with the water in it.

After a lot of water has been splashed on the floor, and you've swept up a few broken glasses, show them how to crisscross the knives into a triangle:

And then balance them on the glasses to complete the trick:

What could be simpler? (Once you've seen the diagram, that is.) Quick! Catch that glass! It's . . . well, never mind.

Geometricks

My youngster caught me shaking his piggy bank the other day—where else are you going to find some change when your wife took all your money shopping, and the mailman won't put postage due on the Diners Club? I was bracing myself, hoping somehow I'd get off with just a tongue lashing, when the kid said, "Never mind, Dad. Help yourself. I already doubled my allowance this week."

"Hmm," I said, immediately interested. "Tell me more." I put my arm around the lad in a fatherly manner, carefully palming just enough change to square me with the U.S. mail. "How does a bright young man double his allowance?"

He showed me how. Somewhere he'd gotten hold of a bunch of simple challenges, most of them based on geometry, and best operated with a little side bet and very little conscience. The fellow who knows the answer arranges the pieces—crayons, pencils, toothpicks, coins, whatever's available—and then challenges the fellow without the answers to change the design a certain way with a simple move or two.

The truth is, they're not as simple as they look. My son stumped me easily on most of them. One of these days I'm going to get even with that kid.

Toothpicketing

Give someone five toothpicks. Ask him to arrange them

to form the number 19. (Don't try this with Latin scholars or Goldwater Republicans. They'll get it every time.)

Here's the answer:

Now give him four more toothpicks, nine in all. Tell him: make 10 out of them. (Since you've just pulled that Roman number routine on him, he'll spend a lot of time trying to add and subtract Xs and Is and do it that way. It's not that hard.)

The answer:

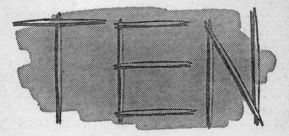

Put six toothpicks in front of your victim . . ., I mean, your friend. Now slip him the challenge: Take these six and make four equal sized triangles.

After he fiddles around awhile, and finally gives up, show him how it's done:

Squaresville

Take twelve toothpicks (but don't take them out of 12 martinis—this is not a game to be played lying under the barstool) and arrange them this way:

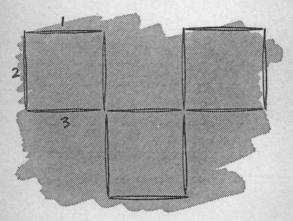

The problem is: by moving only three toothpicks, form five squares.

Here's how:

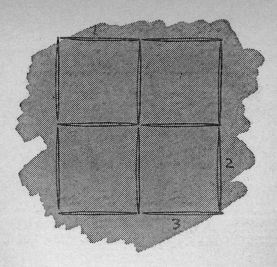

Find the fifth square? The big one, of course.

Don't Do Dot

Put nine dots on a cocktail napkin about a half-inch apart in the form of a simple grid, like this:

Here's the challenge: join all the dots by making only

four straight lines, and without lifting the pen from the paper.

The solution:

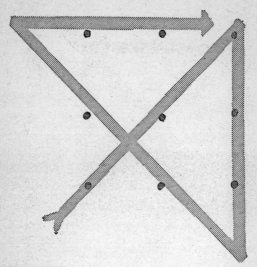

Try that last one again, with a few more dots. Draw out a grid like this:

And ask your friend to connect the 16 dots with only six straight lines, again without lifting the pen from the paper, or retracing. Here's how it's done:

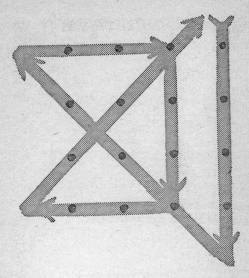

Coinfusion

Try this one. Put a handful of coins out on the bar. Eight, nine, ten . . . loan me a couple of coins. I need a dozen. Then I put them in two rows, see, like this:

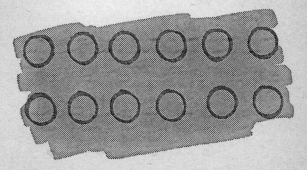

Here's the idea: you ask that guy next door if he can arrange them in six rows, with four coins in each row. Your chances of his failing are a little better, as you can see in the answer below, if he isn't a flagmaker fresh in from Israel.

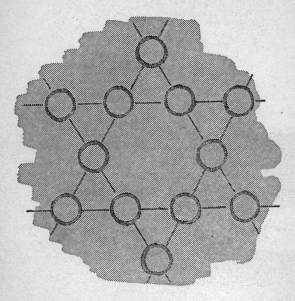

The Infernal Triangle

People have stared at this triangle of coins long enough for a decent beer to go flat without being able to make a simple change: turn it upside down by moving only three coins.

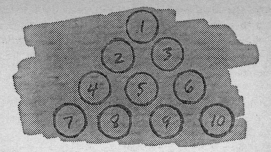

Give up? To save your beer, I'll explain:
1. Move 7 to the left of 2.
2. Move 10 to the right of 3.
3. Move 1 below 8 and 9.
And what do you know? It's upside down:

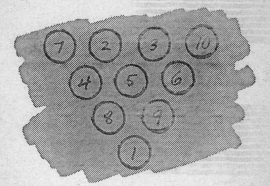

One thing I haven't explained yet about these Betchas. Maybe you already thought of the problem. What if you try one on a guy and someone else has already showed him how to win the challenge?

That's easy. Just bow slightly from the waist, accept defeat gracefully, and buy the man a drink. After all the drinks you've won, you can afford to be gracious about it.

Onioneering

The bartender gave you an onion in your Gibson, although you distinctly said "skip the onion." To illustrate, using toothpicks (or matches, whatever) it looks like this:

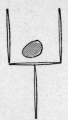

Here's what I want you to do: get that onion on the outside of the glass by moving only two toothpicks—yet still retaining the shape of the cup.

Here's the way:
    Start:

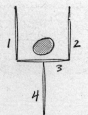

Step 1—move 3 to the left
so that it's under 1:

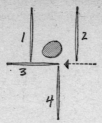

Step 2—move 2 perpendicular
to 3, parallel to 4:

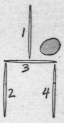

What? Spilled your Gibson? How come you didn't drink
it first?

Games (Drinking)
People Play
Or
Breaking the Ice Is
More Fun Than
Watching It Melt

. . . OK, Bill, if you insist, I'll have another martini. You know, I really don't drink any more. (On the other hand, I don't drink any less, either.) Ahh! That's it. Perfect! You can stir for me any time, Bill. Good olives, too.

Now, you see this toothpick? The wasted woodwork in a martini. Most people think they're just a way to get the olive without skindiving. Actually, the toothpick is one of those things usually wasted around a bar—like bottle caps, loose change and spare time—which can actually be used in a number of worthwhile activities. Here, I'll show you what I mean. Got the time?

Pile-Up Stix

If you get along as well with your favorite mix-master as I do with Bill, he'll let you have a handful of toothpicks to try this next game. (You'll find that most bartenders are terribly generous with everything but the stuff they sell. I still get tears in my eyes when I think of that time in—when was it? 1957? '58? when Bill bought me a drink.) This game consists simply of piling tooth-picks on top of a beer bottle. That's what I said, tooth-picks on a beer bottle! If it sounds so easy, try it!

Two people take turns, and the winner is the one who gets the last toothpick on top of the bottletop before the whole mess falls off—a moment you can dramatize by yelling:

TIMMMBERR R R R R R!

The guy (or the gal) who causes this disaster gets to (1) pick up the toothpicks and (2) buy the next round of beers.

Toothpick Checkers

You have to have two different color toothpicks for this game—maybe four white ones pulled out of martini olives and four colored ones out of hors d'oeuvres. (Or you can borrow them from the bartender, or use matches, if you don't want to take the time to harvest your own.)

Arrange them on a board of rectangles four wide and four deep, with the toothpicks set up like this for the start of the game:

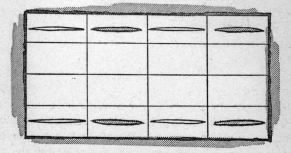

One player has the white toothpicks and the other the colored ones. The players compete to see who can be the first to get his toothpicks in a straight line. The winning line-up can be horizontal, perpendicular, or diagonal, but it must be in one line, and on adjoining squares.

Players take turns, each moving one toothpick. They can go in any direction, but only one square at a time. Unlike checkers, there is no jumping over another player's man.

Line-Up

Line-Up is similar to toothpick checkers, but played on a bigger board, and with bigger men. The playing field is a 25-square grid, and the men are either 10 bottlecaps (half must be turned upside down, or half must be a different brand) or 10 coins of two different sizes and colors (pennies and nickles work fine).

Lay the men down the way they are shown in the picture below, with black and white (shiny and dark) men alternating.

The players take turns, one moving the black, the other the white, going one square at a time forward, backward, sideways in either direction, or kitty-cornered. Again, no jumping. The object of the game is to move the men until one player has all his in a straight row:

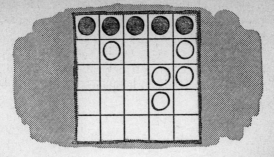

The winning player may get his men in a straight line, up and down, crosswise, or from one corner of the board to the other.

Shufflebar

This is a version of shuffleboard, the favorite game of beer bars and ocean liners. If you're somewhere in-between, and want to play it, anyway, I'll show you how:

Take a couple of sheets of paper (menus work fine) and draw two triangles, splitting each up into three portions, valued 1 through 3. Set them up facing each other, about a barstool apart, and borrow three beer bottle caps apiece to use as weights—that's what they call them aboard the Lurline. The set up:

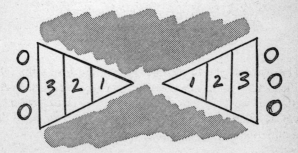

The two players take turns snapping the weights toward the targets with a flick of the flicking finger. You get only one snap per weight. Liners count for the higher value when more than half of the weight is on the high side of the line.

You can also play it right on the bar, if the bartender doesn't mind your drawing triangles on his bartop with a felt tip pen. Bill would never object, but some bartenders might. If they give you any trouble, call the Matson Lines. Or go around the corner to Curly's Place.

Table Hockey

This is another one you can play with coins, at a small table. Three coins are the pucks. For a net a player uses his forefinger and little finger extended over the edge of the table. The opposing player tries to snap the three coins into the net from wherever they land when they are dropped at random on the table. (The player who is being the goalie gets to drop the coins—hoping, of course, that they'll land in the most disadvantageous places on the table.)

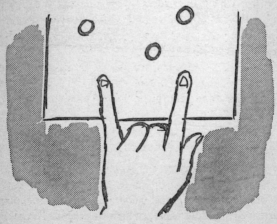

Whoever is shooting gets to keep shooting until a coin either goes off the table (see Plink, page 46) or lands in someone's martini by mistake (see Splink, page 00). Then the player who was goalie gets to shoot. The new goalie drops the coins, and the new shooter starts snapping them toward the net.

Any coin will do. A couple of guys I know were doing it with quarters, but when they were looking around on the floor for one that fell off the table, the barmaid cleared the playing surface of pucks, mistaking them for tips. Thereafter (until the bartender sent them both home for dueling with swizzle sticks) they played with bottle caps.

Splink

Here's a game two can play with little skill, no rules, and a minimum of mental exertion. Next to slapjack, it's my brother-in-law's favorite.

You spread a paper napkin over the top of a glass tumbler, and place a dime in the center. Then, with lighted cigarettes, you and your companion take turns burning holes in the paper around the edge of the glass. The person who burns the hole that causes the dime to drop is the loser—and has to pay for the next round of drinks.

Oh yes, I forgot to mention, the tumbler has to be half full of water. It doesn't affect the playing of the game. But, when the dime falls in, splink! And that's the name of the game.

Plink

If you liked Splink, try this one, it's even simpler. It's great for toward the end of the evening, on those kind of nights when you can get a belly laugh by telling people the bartender's middle name, or shouting, Spiro Agnew!

Two people seated at opposite sides of a small table take turns flicking dimes toward one another's side of the table, trying to see which can get his (or her) dime closest to the edge without it falling off—plink! onto the floor. The dimes are propelled with a snap of the forefinger. Don't worry if you lose a few. They always sweep them up in the morning. (In classy bars, where they have carpet on the floor, this game goes by another name: fffpf.)

Flip

This game takes a deck of cards and a pair of dice, but it has the advantage of being neither a card game nor a regular dice-player's game.

Each player gets a run of cards from 2 to queen, and lays them out, face up, like this:

That gives you one card to match the totals possible in a roll of dice, from 2 up to 12.

The players take turns throwing dice. When you throw, you add up the total shown on the dice, and then turn over the corresponding card. (Roll a 6 and a 4 and you turn over the 10; a pair of 6's and you get to turn over the queen.) Roll a double and you get another turn.

The first player who manages to flip over all his cards wins.

It's a good game for two, but three or four can play, too, with one deck of cards. In fact, one person can play it alone if he—like me—can't stand playing solitaire.

Piggy

The winner in Piggy is the player who first rolls a total of 100 points with a pair of dice. Whoever has the dice can keep on rolling until he gets to 100, without giving the other fellow a chance unless he wants to. Sound piggy? Right! The catch is that the player with the dice loses everything he's added up so far if he rolls a one. Then the second player automatically gets his turn.

He can roll and roll until he either gets to 100, or rolls an ace, in which case the first player goes again.

In practice, it works out like this: I roll until I've got a fair total—let's say 42. Then, fearing a one-spotter, I let you have a chance. I keep my 42 and I can see how well you're doing before I decide how many rolls in a row I want to risk in running my total toward 100.

You'll probably go for broke, hoping to catch up. Maybe you will. Once I got to 98, and I was piggy—I kept the dice for one more roll. Guess what I got? Yep. Snake-eyes! I had my 100, but it didn't count—I was busted back to zero again. Life's like that. So's Piggy.

The Big Pickup

There's no way to lose this one, not if you know the secret. It looks pretty honest to begin with: two players place 15 coins (or 15 toothpicks, or 15 matches) on the bar in front of them. Then they take turns withdrawing from one to three pieces from the pile each turn. The one who has to pick up the last piece loses.

Here's the trick: count the coins the other player takes, and make sure you get the second, sixth and tenth coin to be removed. When you pick up No. 10, you've got it made.

Suppose you get No. 10. The most your opposing player can take is three. If he does pick up three, you take one, No. 14, making him pick up the last one. The least he can take after you get No. 10 is one. So you take three—and again he has to be the one to pick up the last one.

The Big Add-Up

It's hard to lose this one, too. And, furthermore, it has the advantage that it has no moving parts to get out of order—except your head. It's like the Big Pickup, but played without pieces, and with slightly different numbers. The object of the game is to get to the number 20 before your drinking partner does.

Either player starts with 1, and the players take turns adding on either 1 or 2. The one who adds on the number that brings the total to 20 is the winner. For example, if I say 1, you can say 2 or 3. Then I can say 4 or 5. We're on our way to 20—but I'll bet I get there first, knowing the secret:

The idea is to reach 2, 5, 8, 11, 14 or 17 when it comes your turn. If I can get to 17, I've got it made. You can say either 18 or 19. I say 20—and I've won.

Liar's Poker

The eight numbers in the serial number of the dollar bill lend themselves to what goes by the name of Liar's Poker, or, sometimes, Dollar Bill Poker. Next to a trip to Las Vegas, I can't think of a faster way of streamlining your wallet.

What you do is imagine that the digits represent cards, with the 1 an ace. The idea is to make the best poker hand out of the numbers (as though they were cards) in your own and your opponent's hand. Of course, you don't know what he's got in his hand; that's where bluffing comes in. And he doesn't know what's in your hand; that's where lying comes in.

You and your friend each take out a dollar bill, holding it so the other can't see the serial number, and one of you opens the betting. You bet (it's more like bidding) on what you think could be made out of what's in both hands, so if you have three 1s (an unlikely event) you'd probably be safe in saying: "Four aces." Surely he'll have at least one more 1. He has to either top you or call. If he calls, and you've got it, he pays you a buck. But if you can't make it—suppose he doesn't have a 1—you have to pay him a buck.

Of course he can raise the betting, and say, for instance, "Five 4s." Then you have to either top his bet or else call him.

Like poker, this game can be played by several people. When the player next to you doesn't want to call or bid higher, the chance to do so goes on to the next person. The game goes on until nobody wants to risk going any higher. Then everybody turns over their bills, and it's up to the highest bidder (or perhaps the biggest liar) to prove he can find the hand he said he could. Sometimes, in a big crowd like this, it's best to try to be the second biggest liar. Because the fellow who bids big and can't deliver has to pay everybody a buck. Of course, if he can find the hand he predicts, he collects a dollar from everyone there.

As you see, a lot of money can change hands in a hurry this way. Some players save their favorite bills for the next time they play—which is okay if everybody does that, but can be rough on a hapless chap with just run-of-the-mint greenbacks in his pocket. So remember, if your compatriots start searching in the crannies of their billfolds for hidden treasures, you can suggest that dollars, like cards, can be shuffled. They'll probably settle for potluck from bartender Bill's cash drawer.

Bill Banditry

I've seen people sit by the hour playing Liar's Poker, where you gamble on what numbers are on the other guy's dollar bill. Here's a variation that's a lot simpler. And, furthermore, it has the added advantage of being slightly crooked.

There are eight numbers on a dollar bill. The challenge: without looking, pick three numbers out of the eight on any given dollar bill. Your bills, his bills, or some fresh, neutral ones out of the cash register. Three out of eight? Sounds like the odds are better than 2 to 1 in his favor, doesn't it?

Here's how you almost always win: bills with seven or eight different numbers are very rare, and most have only five or six different numbers. I've seen some with only two different numbers. The odds are that someone can successfully predict three numbers on any one bill about once in six tries. Even if you give away 2 to 1 odds you're way ahead.

Suppose he picks 3, 7 and 9. Most bills will look like this: (five different numbers)

| A45580809E |

or like this (six different numbers)

| L62543993A |

so he can't win. You might even get a bill like this (two numbers)

| L53353535A |

And he hasn't got a chance. But suppose he gets this one?

| L86791532E |

My friend, you buy the drinks. But what's wrong with one out of six?

Super Tic-Tac-Toe

Tic-Tac-Toe is a terrible game. It works on a formula, and anyone who knows the formula can beat anyone who doesn't. And just about everyone knows the formula. But have you tried Super Tic-Tac-Toe? It's a bit more complicated, and you'll never meet anyone who knows the formula. Here's how it's played:

Instead of the usual two-line tic-tac-toe grid, draw a four-line grid, like this:

Play it like regular Tic-Tac-Toe. Except at the end of the game you figure the winner by a simple formula:

1 point—3 in a row (in a straight line, horizontal, diagonal or vertical).

2 points—4 in a row.

3 points—5 in a row.

If you'd like, you can play it on a bigger grid. Try it with seven spaces per row. There's only one problem with the bigger board: it's more work counting up after the game is over.

Circle Tic-Tac-Toe

My friend Al actually invented this one: The playing area consists of 4 concentric circles intersected by 8 lines, 45 degrees to each other.

Two players alternate turns filling in an "x" or "o." The object of the game is to place 4 consecutive "x's" or "o's" in either a circular or vertical row. Three possible winning combinations are illustrated in the diagram.

Too complicated for you? Try it a couple of times. You may wind up going around in circles—just like Al.

Pickled Picasso

Here's one that sounds easy, but it isn't. Have your game partner draw a picture of whatever it is that you describe—something from your pocket, perhaps, or, if your partner's a lady, her purse. Try your cuff link. Describe to your friend what it looks like, without letting him (or her) see it, and without naming any of its parts. (Come to think of it, who knows the names for the parts of a cuff link, anyway?) While you describe it, the other person draws a picture of it—and then has to guess what it is from the picture. It's not easy. Would you believe this is what one sweet young thing said was a cuff link?

This game also gives you some interesting insights into strangers. Tells you what they've got in their pockets and purses. At a party, at one woman's directions, I drew something which came out this way:

"I'll be darned," I said, "if it doesn't look like a frog!" "Absolutely wrong," she said, sneaking whatever it was back into her purse. "It's a prince." She was just putting me on, I think. But why was she wearing that black outfit and that funny pointed hat?

Parking Lot

Did the guy who parked your car in the lot outside drive like he warmed up for the night's work in a Destruction Derby on Wide World of Sports? The attendant got out of my car one time—what was left of my car—and told me: "If you can walk away from it, it's a good parking." It so happens there's a game based on this sport. It's called Parking Lot. Want to bend some fenders? Here's how it goes:

It takes two game boards—we'll call them that, even though the back of a cocktail napkin will do. Each player lays out a grid of 25 squares, five by five. The grids are numbered down the left side, lettered across the top, just like those filling station maps you can never get to stay folded.

Each player hides his board from the other, and then fills in four spaces, all together but in any direction, labeling them to represent his own car. Each car takes up four spaces—Ford, Chev, Linc, Cadd, whatever abbreviations you like.

The game boards for a Ford and a Chevrolet might look like this:

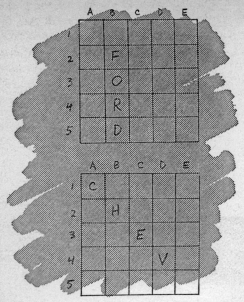

The two players call off spaces, alternately, without being able to see where they're hitting. Your opponent calls off C3, for instance. Take your board, go down from C, over from 3, and draw an X where the space is. (On the boards above, this would've missed the Ford, but creamed the Chevvy just behind the door.) When your opponent calls out the shot, he marks an O on his own board, so he won't call out the same space over again.

To win you have to hit all four spaces of your opponent's car. When you score a hit, he has to tell you, so you know about where to try next time. But, of course, you don't know which direction his car is parked, so you don't know whether to try to the left, right, top, or bottom of the first hit. It takes a lot of groping around to wipe out the other guy's car. And, in the meantime, he might just get yours.

Want more room to play on? Real estate isn't so ex-

pensive that you can't double the size of the parking lot
—and, if you've got a little more time, double the fun.
More people can play, too, and you can throw in a
Honda (just a lone "H") for the cocktail waitress. A
Honda, taking up only one space, is a hard target. (But,
Bill tells me, so is the cocktail waitress.) For a parking lot
more like the one at Belmont Park, try one with 1 to 10
down the side and A to J along the top.

City Blocks

Turn your cocktail napkin over. Take a pen and make
five dots across the top, then five more down the sides.
Then fill in the dots until you've got a grid of 25. It
ought to look like this:

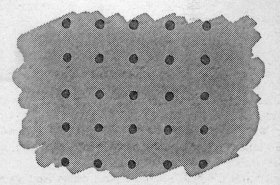

You ask the other player to draw a line connecting two of the dots. You draw one at right angles to it. If he puts another parallel to it, you connect it across the open side, making a box. Then you put your initial in it, and explain: you've just won a box. And the player who wins the most boxes wins the game.

This game is called City Blocks. It goes fast—a line, a line, a line, then a box, almost as fast as you can draw lines. But there's a little more skill than meets the eye, as you'll discover when you've tried it a couple of times.

The point is that at the same time you are trying to complete a box, you are trying not to fill in the third line —which will allow the other player to complete his box.

Exasperation
My friend Al, who showed me this one, calls it Cinch.

But—the son of a gun!—he wouldn't tell me how it's done. He laid it out like this:

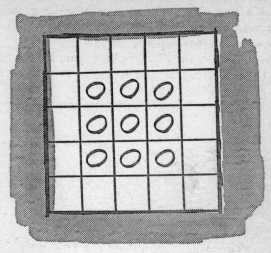

And then told me what I had to do:

Get all the coins off the board by jumping one coin over another—across, up, down and diagonally, as in checkers. You may use the same coin to jump over more than one man, like a run in checkers. And, as in checkers, when you jump a man, take him off the board. However, —and here's the catch—the last coin must wind up in the center square.

Al did it jump-jump-jump, like the checker champion of the Volunteer Fire Department. "It's a cinch," he said. I've been trying for a year to figure it out. Can you? (I didn't say this book had all the answers, did I?)

Coaster Flip

Balance a coaster (the kind made out of cork or heavy cardboard) on the edge of the bar, so about half of it is sticking over the edge. Take your hand, palm down, and come up under the coaster, flipping it up into the air—and catching it with the same hand.

One isn't hard. Try it with two, then three—and you'll be busy as a seven-ball juggler on the old Keith Circuit.

Whoever snatches the most coasters out of the air—before one skims into that fat lady's decolletage—wins the game.

Bucking Up

Bucking Up, sometimes called odds or evens, is less simple than it sounds. Two players put out either one or two fingers, and take turns guessing whether the total displayed will be either an odd or an even number. The total on a given throw will thus have to be two, three or four.

It may not be immediately apparent, but there's more than the odds of chance to deal with here. You also have to take into consideration what you think I'm going to throw down, what I think you think I'm going to throw down, and what I think you're going to think about what you think I'm going to throw . . .

In other words, it's as complicated as the guy (or gal) you're playing it with. Figure in advance how many points make a game.

The Old Italian Finger Fling

This game was invented by an old Italian, but, since it should be played fast and noisily, it is actually best for young Italians. Or young anyone elses. Let's try it. Here's how: I throw out a number of fingers, one to five, and so do you. I don't know what you're going to throw, and you don't know how many I'm going to throw. Simultaneously, we call out what we guess will be the total number of fingers played. Sometimes nobody wins. Do it again, faster! Make your guess—SIX! NINE —louder! Argue a lot over what the score is! FIVE! EIGHT! Bang your glasses on the bar!

And remember that old Italian saying: "I've been thrown out of better bars than this!"

What's the Good
Word?
Or
Scrambled Sayings,
Swifties, Hink Dinks
and Beyond

The kind of games I like best are those which require as the only specialty that simple old Gaelic facility, talking. Word games. This next category consists of fun you can have with words—plus a little imagination. With most of them you don't even have to write anything down, unless you've come up with something so damned clever you want to write it down so you'll remember it later, when you're stone sober. I know a guy who tried that, but he gave it up. "It's not the same the next day," he said, soberly. Oops! I just slipped in a Swifty. What's a Swifty? Well, it's sort of like a Hink Dink, but . . . well, if you really want to find out, my friend, read on.

Swifties

Tom Swift was the hero of the kids' books who performed all those intrepid deeds in his electric dirigible, flying motorcycle, and lead balloon, while modifying his dialogue with an adverb. Remember? "Who says I can't go over Niagara Falls in a barrel?" asked Tom, bravely.

Punsters with a tendency to the adverbial (the very

worst kind) ran wild with what became known as Swifties. They make a good challenge for a barside companion— first you think of one, then it's the other guy's (or gal's) turn. Here are a few to get your imagination stirred:

From showbiz:

"Make mine a martini," said Martin, dryly.

"May I have this dance?" asked Fred Astaire, gingerly.

"What wise guy stole my toupee?" cried Jack Benny, distressedly.

"I enjoy living in Switzerland," said the tax-free film star, evasively.

"I'd love to make another 'Road' picture," said Bing Crosby, hopefully.

Historically speaking:

"Good morning, Julius," said Brutus, cuttingly.

"This is the end," said Cleopatra, venemously.

From modern times:

"I simply love to pose for pictures," Miss Playboy bare-ly murmured.

"I had trouble with my power saw," he said offhanded-ly.

"I'll have your coffee right away, dear," she said, instantly.

Or:

"There's no more Tom," he said, glancing over the falls, swiftly.

Hink Dinks and Beyond

Hink Dink is a guessing game that rhymes. "What," you ask, "is a self effacing secret agent?" An old Hink Dink player will get the answer in a moment: "A shy spy." Then he gets to try one on you—or, perhaps, to go on to a Hinky Dinky. A Hinky Dinky has two words of two syllables, and rhymes. For experts, there's the Hinkity Dinkity: two words of three syllables. And still rhyming.

The best way to explain Hink Dinks, etc., is by giving you a few examples. You can make up others, just by looking around the room, or glancing at a newspaper. Here are a few for starters:

Hink Dinks
A precision derision .... a fab jab.
A smelly, inebriated mammal .... a drunk skunk.
A healer's affliction .... a doc's pox.
A modest dentifrice .... a chaste paste.
An airlifted biscuit .... a flown scone.

Hinky Dinkies
An ineffectual heavy drinker .... a loser boozer.
An unattractive couple .... a gruesome twosome.
Malodorous TV (British) .... smelly telly.
An irascible dieter .... a ratty fatty.

Hinkity Dinkities
A Spanish dictionary .... a Mexican lexicon.
A highly recommended cure .... a terrific specific.
An evil clergyman .... a sinister minister.
A sharp putdown .... a precision derision.
        Anyone for a Hinkidity Dinkidity? Or a Hinkidickity Dinkidickity? Or a couple of aspirin, maybe?

Word Squares
Each player lays out a 5-by-5 grid, 25 squares in all. Players take turns calling out letters. Players try to arrange the letters in the grid to make words. Each player uses both his own and the other player's letters. The aim of the game is to make as many words as possible—arranged vertically, horizontally, and if you're very sharp, diagonally. Words inside words count, too. Each player gets as many points as there are letters in the words he's made by the time all the squares in the grid are filled.

Halfway through, your grid might look like this:

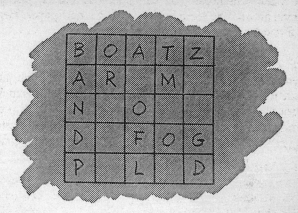

You've got boat and oat, and inside oat you've got at, too. Catch that diagonal, brood? (Note that letters can be repeated.) Knowing how, you can offer letters that make words-within-words like train (rain, in), grate (rate, ate, at) and every (very, eve). Your opponent will soon learn to do the same. And, by the way, this is one puzzle it's safe to do in ink. You can't move letters once they're in place.

Mate Mixing

"I'm going to have a party," you explain, "and I'm going to invite Bertrand and Rosalind Russell. Who do you want to invite?"

It has to be a mismatched couple, of course. A fast thinker will probably be able to think up a couple to add to the invitation list: "Tennessee and Esther Williams."

A friend of mine who can't spell invited Burt and Elsa Lanchester. A few other popular couples at these mixed-up parties: Fess and Suzy Parker, Steve and Butterfly McQueen, Holden and Joan Caulfield.

If you want to relax the rules and say it doesn't have to be a man and a woman, the couples can get even wilder. There's Colonel and George Sanders, Senator and Audie Murphy, Maury and Chill Wills. A Laugh-In fan wanted to bring Judy and Chili Con Carne and Beautiful Downtown and Luther Burbank.

But you have to draw the line somewhere. What kind of a party could you have where someone brought Oil Leaks Off and Dinah Shore?

Double Trouble

Similar to Mate Mixing is Double Trouble—where it's the initials that count, and the second member of the pair has to have initials which are the reverse of those of the first one. A good Double Trouble pair: Betty Hutton and Harry Belafonte.

There are those who'll want to play this game by starting at the letter A and going straight through to Z, but—since there's only one Zavier Cugat—I recommend against it. Also, before you start, you have to decide how many Double Trouble pairs it takes to make a game, and what the time limit is. And do they have to be a man and a woman, or not? For man-and-woman players, there are fewer combinations. Some of those available: Margaret Sanger and Sal Mineo; Richard Burton and Bobo Rockefeller; Garson Kanin and Kate Greenaway.

But look at all the pairs you can pair if you aren't worried about the sexes: Edward Albee and Alfred Einstein; Lyndon Johnson and Jack Lemmon; Pierre Salinger and Sidney Poitier; Vivien Leigh and Lupe Velez; Zachary Scott and Efrem Zimbalist.

Want to make the game even easier? Then allow the substitution of any well-known two-word phrase for names. That way you can put together Tom Dewey and Dial Tone. I don't like it myself, but that's one of the curses of the Irish. We're purists.

Double Words

"Strip poker!" I say, and the game begins. But it isn't played with cards, and you can keep your clothes on. It's just the first double word I threw out for you to match with another double word—one beginning with the word mine ended with. You could say: "poker face." And I'd have to come up with something like "face powder." From there we would go to "powder magazine" to "magazine subscription." The game ends when the other person can't think of a double word within a specified period of time. Thirty seconds? Ten seconds? You decide.

Several people can play the game. If you want, start with five people, and cut the time limit to five seconds. The slow thinkers will soon be over in the corner muttering double dirty words.

Scrambled Sayings

With just a little courage—well, on second thought, let's say quite a little courage—you can stump your friends with Scrambled Sayings. You give them a story. They have to guess the punch line. In each case it's a saying (or a theft, perhaps, from a song) which may have been altered a bit. Let me show you how it's done. First, I'll tell you the story:

Hearing that a British warship was approaching his island, and afraid of being robbed, a native king stowed his pearl-encrusted throne away in the attic of his thatched hut. But, when the warship fired its cannon in a salute, the roof poles snapped, and the heavy chair fell on the king, killing him.

That's the story. What does it prove?

People who live in grass houses shouldn't stow thrones.

Now, if I'd've wanted to help you, I could've given you a few hints about the saying, such as, "It starts, People

67

who . . ." It depends on how much Christian charity (or any other kind) you wish to scatter around.

You might try some of your friends (preferably the nonviolent ones) with this one:

A man brings home what the pet shop owner tells him is a perfect pet, a rary. The rary doesn't eat, drink, wet, mess, or make a sound. He is furry and lovable, and has big brown eyes. But the perfect pet, in time, shows one serious fault: it keeps growing. First it's the size of a cat, then a dog, a pony, a Percheron horse, a small elephant —and getting bigger. Finally, when his garage is bursting at the seams from the size of his rary, the owner decides he'll have to drop him into the quarry at the edge of town—where the rary, needing neither food nor drink, can grow as large as he wants. The man rents a big dump truck, coaxes the affectionate, trusting rary aboard, drives him to the quarry, backs up to the edge of a 100-foot drop, and begins to tilt the bed of the dump truck up. The rary looks down at the bottom of the quarry, and, as he begins slipping slowly out of the dump truck, he turns his big, brown eyes on his owner, and utters his first sound.

What does he say?

That's a long, long way to tip a rary.

Assuming you still have an audience, try them on a good, old fashioned missionary story:

Brother Paul and Brother Matthew, two missionaries, are trapped and caught by Indians. The chief tells them that the only way they can be saved from the stake is if they can match the ability of the tribe's most skillful spear thrower. This warrior, from 50 feet, cuts in half a piece of snail-shell wampum so tiny it takes 10 of them to equal a white man's dollar. Old Brother Paul knows he can't do it, so he turns to his younger companion, and asks: (All right, you asked for it)

Brother, can you spear a dime?

Or—and this could be just the hint that your listeners need—perhaps it's a good night for a knight story:

Sir Osgood's horse stumbles and dies after a battle, and Sir Osgood, finally able to walk no farther, throws his arms around the neck of his old mastiff hound. The mastiff, wet, cold and bedraggled, drags him to the door of a castle, where he barks until the owners come. The owner's wife insists they can't let a stranger into the castle. "But," says the owner of the castle, "I. . . ."

All right. But what?

"But," he says, "I wouldn't put a knight out on a dog like this."

The fire-breathing dragon traps Sir Humbert, Sir Phillpott and their page and is about to devour them, when the ugliest witch they've ever seen suddenly appears and calls him off.

"Promise me a trunk full of gold," she says, "or I'll sic my dragon on you."

The dragon belches fire ominously. "Tell her yes," whispers Sir Phillpott. "Yes, yes," cries Sir Humbert. "Two trunks full. But turn off that damned flamethrower."

"And," adds the witch, "I need a wagonload of bats, frogs and lizards. My spice cabinet is about empty."

"I'll send them," says Sir Humbert. "I promise."

"And lastly," says the witch, cackling with delight, "one of you has to stay behind—and become my husband."

Sir Phillpott turns to Sir Humbert, and whispers:

Okay. What is it he whispers?

"Promise her anything. But give her our page."

See what I mean about this game calling for a little courage? There's a rumor Wild Bill Hickock was shot in the back just after he told that last story. I wouldn't try one of these if you're holding aces and eights.

. . . what's that, Bill? A scrambler I forgot? The foo bird? Of course, the foo bird! It goes like this: there was a safari, and the white hunter warns the other members that the natives consider it a bad omen to wipe away stains left by the legendary foo bird. Well, one day. . . .

Never mind. Here comes the barmaid. I'll tell you some other day. Or can you already guess?

The Numbers Games
Or
How to Add and
Subtract
Your Way To
Success

Nothing amazes non-mathematical types more than a numbers game. I'm not the kind of guy who can balance a bank statement, and I was surprised when I found out that I could work a lot of these numbers games as well as my friend Al, the computer wizard, who showed me how to do them.

Her Innermost Secrets! Yours! Now!

The kind of trick which begins, "Take a number from one to ten, double it and add . . ." has been with us a long, long time. It is based, in fact, on a simple mathematical formula which appears to be quite complex and magical. For example, you ask a friend to pick a number, any number, and tell you what it is. Then, if he will just follow some easy arithmetic, you will make him arrive at that same number. Let's say he comes up with 27 as the number you must get to. Then ask him to write down (without letting you see):

1. Any number from 1 to 99
   (This time without letting you know)   35

2. Double it	70
3. Add 12	82
4. Divide by 2	41
5. Subtract the original number (35)	

At this point, according to the formula, no matter what number he picked in step 1, the answer to step 5 will always be six! (Try it yourself.) The rest is child's play, but quite effective. You can get him to 27 in several ways:

| 6. Add 29 | 35 |
| 7. Subtract 8 | 27! |

—OR . . .

| 6. Double it | 12 |
| 7. Add 15 | 27! |

—OR . . .   (If you're in a hurry)

| 6. Add 21 | 27! |

Now you see how it's done. There are other mathematical tricks, all relatively simple once you've mastered the formula. I've had lots of fun with them—though perhaps not in quite the same way as my friend Al, who is, as I told you, in computers. His way may be of interest to you. Try it on that little redhead you've been eyeing at the next table.

Al starts out by saying something which piques the young lady's curiosity, like, "It's truly amazing what a few numbers can tell us." "Like what?" she is guaranteed to ask. "With a few numbers," you say, "I can tell a woman how many times she's been married, how many times she's been engaged, and how many guys got away." "Like how?" she'll query. At this point, Al says, you eye her steadily, whip out the old ballpoint, and give her the back of an envelope to write on. "Like this," you say:

Ask her to write down, without showing you:

1. The number of times she's been married (three times, let's say)
   3
2. Then you tell her to multiply by 2
   6
3. Add 3
   9
4. Multiply by 5
   45
5. Then ask her to add the number of times engaged (again, three times)
   48
6. Multiply by 10
   480
7. Add those who got away (or better still, ones she's turned down. Two, in this case)
   482
8. Finally, she should subtract 150
   332
9. And multiply by 2
   664

Now, ask her for the figure she's arrived at. When you get it, divide by two (thus cancelling out step nine, which was mere camouflage, anyway). The answer to step eight (332) supplies you with all the vital information:

First digit: the number of times she's been married (3)

Second digit: the number of times she's been engaged (3)

Third digit: the number of guys she's turned down (2)

This trick, incidentally, always works except if the young lady has been either married, engaged, or otherwise been involved with more than nine fellas. And if that's the case, maybe you should forget the whole thing.

Did you get her attention, at least? According to Al, you're on your way. While she's trying to figure it—and you—out, here's another. (The real trick is to keep moving at all times.) Be advised that this one may be a little dangerous. Through more mathematical magic, you are about to tell the young lady her age!

Ask her to write down (no peeking):

1. Her age (24, say. That's a nice round number) 24
2. Multiply by three 72
3. Add one 73
4. Multiply by three again 219
5. Add her age again 243
6. Double it 486

Ask her what this comes to, divide by two (step six is bogus, for purposes of deception), drop the last digit, and you have the answer. But, as before, don't stop there. "Add your shoe size, my dear," you say, "but don't tell me what it is. Ah, what dainty feet . . ." (And if you can throw in a W.C. Fields impression, so much the better.) Finally, you smile and say: "Twenty-four years."

By this time, you're ready for another martini. And so, hopefully, is she.

". . . What's that, Bill? You saw Al the other day and he had a black eye and a piece of tape holding his pipe together? I'm not surprised. I knew someday some girl would write down her real age—and Al would tell her. When in doubt a really smart guy will knock off five years in a hurry. So what if he's wrong? The little lady'll love him for it."

74

Groping

A bachelor I know does a lot of groping around—this story isn't going to end the way you think it is, but keep on reading—and he has to get up early, when it's still dark, and his bedroom light is always burning out.

So he's always groping around in his drawer, trying to find things in the dark. Perhaps you can help him figure out how long he has to hunt to find . . .

Socks

All the socks in his drawer are either blue or black, because that way it's easier for him to find a matching pair. The question is: how many socks does he have to pull out of his drawer in the dark to make sure he has at least one matching pair?

—Only three. Because among those three, there has to be at least one pair of matching socks.

Gloves

In another drawer this chap has 100 gloves. (Bachelors, my friends, are not without their peculiarities.) Once again it is pitch black dark, and he has to reach into the drawer—and remove enough gloves, one by one, until he is sure he has a matching left and right. How many gloves will he have to pull out to get a complete pair?

—To be sure, 51. (Theoretically, he could have pulled fifty lefts or fifty rights.)

Candy

In still another drawer my friend has one of those big demijohns of hard candies. Each piece of candy is the same size and shape, but there are five different flavors.

The problem is, how many individual pieces of candy will we have to take out of the jar in the dark to be sure of getting three of one kind?

—Eleven. After 10 he'd have at least two of each kind. By 11 he'd be sure to have three of one kind. (Raspberry, hopefully. They're his favorite.)

Gridmath

The classic tic-tac-toe grid can also be used for a numbers test—the kind that's just tough enough to figure out. The challenge: arrange the numbers 1 to 9 in the nine spaces below so that they add up to fifteen . . . horizontally, vertically and diagonally.

After a while, you might want to give a clue or two.

Clue 1. Since the number 5 is halfway between 1 and 9, it might make good sense to put it in the center space. (It makes, in fact, very good sense.)

Still struggling? Give them another, a gift.

Clue 2. Try placing the even numbers (2,4,6 and 8) in the corners.

Got it yet? The grid will look like this:

Add it up. It works! But you probably figured it out for yourself ages ago.

Odds or Even?

Don't I hear a lot of change jingling in your pocket? Then split them up, about half in each hand. Now take a look, without telling me. Remember which hand has the even-numbered number of coins and which has the odd. And, in a moment, I'll tell you which is which. Here's how:

1. Multiply the number of coins in your right hand by two. (Say it's 5. That gives you 10.)
2. Multiply the number of coins in the left hand by three. (Say you've got 6. That gives you 18.)
3. Add the totals together and tell me the sum. (28)

With this I can tell you: the even number of coins are in your left hand!

Here's the secret:

If the sum of the two numbers is odd, the left hand has the odd coins. If the sum of the numbers is even, the left hand has the even number of coins.

Counting the Spots

Roll a pair of dice where I can't see them. Even without looking at them—and even if they aren't my dice—and I can tell you what you rolled. That is, I can if you help me a little.

What you have to do is:

1. Roll the dice (let's say it came out 3 and 4)
2. Multiply either one of them by 2 (2 times 4 is 8)
3. Add 1 (making the figure 9)
4. Multiply by 5 (giving you 45)

5. Add what's on the other die, and tell me what you've got. (45 plus 3 is 48)

Then I do a step I don't tell you about: I subtract 5, getting 43. There's the answer: 4 and 3. But when I give you the answer, I'll reverse it—making it 3 and 4—so you won't realize that the 4 in the 48 was part of the giveaway.

(If you had started with 3, it would still work: 2 times 3 is 6. 6 plus 1 makes 7; multiplied by 5 equals 35. Plus what's on the other die (4) gives you 39. Now, subtract 5, and you get 34, or 3 and 4).

Counting the House

Some bars have a leather cup and a pair or two of dice for throwing for drinks. Before you throw another round, build a little house of dice four high, like this:

Now bet someone you know what the total of the numbers on the top and bottom of each of the dice will come to. For four dice, it's 28.

If you have six dice, and they'll stack up that high, the answer is 42. You know why? Not many people are aware of it, but the total of the opposite sides of any die always come to 7. And the total for tops and bottoms of any pile of dice is going to be 7 times however many dice you stacked.

The False Coin

Imagine you have nine coins, one of which is counterfeit, identical to the others except in weight. You have a scale—the old fashioned balancing kind Blind Justice uses in practicing her haphazard profession. Here's the question: in only two weighings, how do you tell which of the nine coins is counterfeit?

If you want to, you can actually work this out by making a scale out of a ruler and a salt cellar, and using eight pennies and a nickel. Everyone would be able to see which is the odd coin, of course. But the question is, how, logically, can you pick it out—in only two weighings?

Like this: first divide the coins into three piles, and weigh any two of the piles. (The counterfeit is shown here as black.)

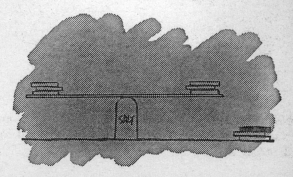

The scale is even; hence you know the odd coin is in the third pile. Had one side been heavier than the other (we're assuming the false coin is heavier) then we'd know the counterfeit was in that pile.

Next we weigh any two of the three coins from the suspect pile. If the coins are even, we know immediately the third one we didn't weigh is spurious. And if one is heavier than the other (as below) we've already done it: the false coin has been found.

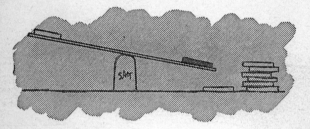

Of course, it's harder to work this out if you're blindfolded.

The Medicine Man's Dilemma

Chief Big Numbers (so named because, as you will see, his store of lore somehow included fractions) was about to die. He told the tribe's medicine man he wanted his most prized possessions—his 11 horses—to be divided among his three sons in the following manner:

No. 1 son, the oldest, was to get half the horses.

No. 2 son, the middle son, was to receive one-fourth the horses.

No. 3 son, the youngest, was to get one-sixth the horses.

He then left promptly for the Happy Hunting Ground, leaving the medicine man to solve the problem.

Can you?

Here's how he did it:

He borrowed another horse from another chief, making 12 horses altogether. Then he divided them this way:

No. 1 son was given six horses (half of the 12).

No. 2 son was given three. (One-fourth of the 12.)

No. 3 son got two (one-sixth of the horses).

That adds up to 11. The twelfth horse, borrowed from the chief, was then returned. And everyone rode away happily into the sunset.

Ah, Sweet Mysteries
of Life
Or
So You Want to be a
Detective

Everybody likes to play detective. When you're having friends over for a few drinks, an easy way to give them the opportunity is by telling what might be called "situation mysteries." The stories involve the whole group and, sooner or later, somebody comes up with the right answer—frequently several people shouting and screaming at the same time. It's a lot of fun.

Take this story:

Two lawyers are having a drink. They hear a car crash and rush outside to see what happened. The first lawyer says, "Oh, my God, that's my wife!" Whereupon, the second lawyer pulls out a gun and shoots the first lawyer.

The question is: What happened? Your listeners ask questions to which you can only answer Yes or No. See if they can figure out the answer:

The second lawyer is a woman—in love with the first lawyer (and with a very low boiling point). Obviously, she was unaware that he was married.

Want to try some more? Try these. In each case it's a question of . . .

What happened?

Mr. Smith walks into a bar and requests a glass of water. The bartender pulls out a gun and points it at him. Mr. Smith smiles, says "Thank you," and then walks out.

What happened?

—Mr. Smith had the hiccups, for which he sought the glass of water. The bartender instead scared the hiccups out of him by pulling the gun. Of course, Mr. Smith smiled: he was grateful.

A man is found dead, hanging from the ceiling with a noose around his neck, in a room which contains absolutely no furniture. His feet are dangling a foot from the floor. There is no one else in the room, which was locked from the inside. Near his feet there is a puddle of water.

What happened?

—The man has committed suicide by jumping off a large block of ice. That explains the puddle of water—the ice melted.

A man is running toward home. Suddenly he encounters a masked man. He quickly stops and begins running back where he started.

What happened?

—It's all taking place at a baseball game. The baserunner is running from third base to home, and is met by a catcher wearing his catcher's mask. The runner stops and races back to third.

A man leaves his house in the morning, kisses his wife goodbye, drives halfway to work, and suddenly turns around, goes back to his house, enters, gets a gun from his desk drawer, and walks into the bedroom and shoots his wife's lover.

What happened?

—While he was driving to work he was listening to his

car radio, and, on one of those call programs, heard the announcer call his home—and a man answered.

Problems of logic also arise in these other story games, although you have to tell me more than just what happened. Read on, and you'll see what I mean.

Outfoxing the Inquisitor

In the days of the Spanish Inquisition, when a Christian boy was found dead, the High Inquisitor falsely accused a rabbi of the murder. He told the rabbi he would leave the matter of guilt or innocence up to heaven—by drawing lots: on one slip of paper he would write guilty, and on the other innocent, and the rabbi would have to make the selection himself.

Here's the rabbi's problem: he knows the High Inquisitor is so anxious to prove him guilty that he'll put guilty on both slips.

How can the rabbi save himself? What would you do?

The rabbi grabs one of the slips of paper and quickly swallows it. Then he asks the rest of the judges to examine the other slip of paper. The remaining slip says guilty. "So," says the rabbi, "that proves that the one I selected was the one that said innocent."

Some people ask: suppose the High Inquisitor hadn't written out two guilties? Well, the rabbi and I figure it this way: he's got to pick one of the two, either way, hasn't he? So what's he got to lose?

Highway Ribaldry

Taxis can be hard to find in Las Vegas. That's what caused a crisis for a friend of mine—a Hollywood chap, as you'll soon see—whose problem might be converted into a game. It would go like this:

He can't find a taxi, and has to use a golf cart to move his party from the Riviera to Caesar's Palace late one night. The golf cart will carry only two at a time, and he's the only one who knows how to run it.

His party is a typical movie crowd—himself, his wife, his beautiful mistress and a notorious gigolo. (Later, in a letter to Dear Abby, I think he explained that it was his wife's idea to bring the gigolo along. She was rich, or something.) Here's the problem:

If he leaves the gigolo and his wife behind together, they'll disappear into the Riviera and perhaps never be seen again.

If he leaves his wife and the mistress behind together, they might well discover that they have something in common. Him.

In fact, the only ones he can leave together are the mistress and the gigolo, who, being more or less professionals, aren't going to be up to anything worse than comparing a few notes.

So how is he going to get this party to Caesar's Palace? If he leaves the mistress and the gigolo alone, fine. But then he'll have to come back for one or the other—and, then, leave him or her with his wife long enough to make the last trip. And that'll be too long.

Try working it out. Tear a couple of business cards in half, label them for the four participants, and see if you can shift them back and forth along the Strip (a foot of Formica bar top will do) until they're all safely at Caesar's Palace.

Give up? Here's how my friend handled it:

1. He took his wife to Caesar's Palace, leaving the gigolo and the mistress alone.

2. Then he returns alone, picks up the gigolo, and takes him there. But, instead of leaving the gigolo with his wife, he takes his wife back with him to the Riviera.

3. Then he leaves his wife in the lobby of the Riviera, and takes the mistress back with him to Caesar's Palace.

4. Leaving the gigolo and the mistress to compare notes —a harmless pastime—he returns alone for his wife, brings her back to join the party.

And he's ready for the midnight show. Life's like that in the Far West. Complicated.

It's All Relative

Ever have trouble trying to figure out how you're related to your wife's aunt's cousin's husband? Or how you can get out of it? (My wife had a cousin by marriage once removed, until the Internal Revenue Service got involved, making him twice removed.) People with big families invariably do better at straightening out kinships than those from small families. In most big families there s a maiden aunt who spends a lot of time keeping the genealogy straight, and she's the one who can tell you whose cousin whose cousin is, and of what degree. So it's for the survivors of the word's big families, and especially their maiden aunts, that I offer these complex relationships for clarification:

A tall Indian and a short Indian stand side by side. The small Indian was the tall Indian's son, but the tall Indian wasn't the short Indian's father. Who was the tall Indian?

—The small Indian's mother.

In a certain group there were two fathers and two sons, yet there were only three people. Who were these strange people?

—A grandfather, a father and a son.

What relationship to you is your brother-in-law's wife's grandmother's husband?

—He's your grandfather!

Can a man marry his widow's sister in the United States?

—Nope. Nor anywhere else. To marry his widow's sister he'd have to be dead.

A man looks at a picture and recites this little poem:
"Brothers and sisters have I none,
Yet this man's father is my father's son."
Whose picture is he looking at?

—His son's.

Under what circumstances could you become your own grandfather?

—Marry a widow with a grown daughter, have your father marry your stepdaughter, and your father thus becomes your son-in-law. But he'll also be your uncle, because he is the brother of your stepmother.

Now, if your father's wife also gives birth to a son, he will be your brother. But he will also be your grandson, because he is the son of your daughter-in-law.

And so—you've followed me this far, I'm sure—here's what happens: as the brother of my own grandchild, my wife (that widow who started this whole mess) becomes my grandmother. And, as the husband of my wife, what does that make me? My own grandfather!

Let's Have a Psych-in

Or

The Doctor Is In

My Aunt Emma used to say you don't have to drink and smoke and hang out in a bar to have a good time, and she was right. You can drink and smoke and hang out at my place, where I've got a great rumpus room with a fireplace and a mini-bar stocked with low-cal vermouth for my own special, nonfat martinis.

And, once we get a few people together, I can show you how to hold a psych-in—where I tell a story, the listeners interpret it, and then I interpret them by their answers. I suppose you could play these games in a bar —especially if you're snowbound—but they take a little time.

You don't have to be a licensed head shrinker to use Dr. Mac's unpatented Insight Inciters. (The only reason they aren't patented is that I stole them from the experts who invented them. Or did I steal them from the guys who stole them from the experts?) Of course, the keys to these stories—and, in one case, a set of pictures—come from the experts. But, as you try them, you'll probably realize that there's more common sense in them than psychology, anyway.

Dream Garden, Anyone?
See that brunette down there at the third seat? What

do you think is going on under that bouffant hairdo? Want to risk trying to find out? (As an older, wiser man, I ought to warn you: it might be a mistake. I don't like the way she peels the top layer off a Gibson onion before she eats it.) But if you're game, ask her these questions —and then let us consider her answers:

1. Tell me what your dream garden would look like.

(Her dream garden shows the front she wants to show the world. Is it neat, orderly, well trimmed? Wild and natural and tangled? Adorned with costly fountains, statuary and pools? If things are just bursting into bloom and full flower, it shows she's probably just bubbling over with health and vitality.)

2. What does the house look like in relation to the garden?

(The garden is her front, but the house—that's the girl herself. How her house relates to her garden shows how she relates to the world. Does her house open out into the garden, or is it above it, hidden from it, or shut off from it?)

3. What would you do if you found out you'd lost the key to your house and wanted to get in right away?

(Or, in other words, what would she do in a case of a crisis? It shows, too, how she might handle a crisis in a friendship. Would she try to climb in a window herself? Call her father or a landlord—some superior being—to make things right? Pray? Curse? Cry? Go spend the night with someone else?)

4. Next to your garden is a fairly high wall surrounding the neighbor's property. There's a gate there but it is locked, and you don't have the key to the lock. You'd like very much to see what's inside. What do you do?

(This time it's a crisis over how she'd behave toward something of someone else's. Would she peek through the keyhole? Try and find something to climb up on to see over? Just climb a tree and jump down, without giving any thought to how she'd get back? Or would she just wait, figuring, with time, she'd find a way?)

5. You've finally gotten into your house. A butler walks up to you and asks you if you'd like a drink? What do you say?

(Sure, it's her house, but where did that butler come from? How much self assurance is she going to show when he asks if she'd like to have a drink? Highly self-assured people will say: "A double martini, stirred, not shaken, and very dry." Those who lack self assurance will say: "Oh, I'll get it myself," or, "How can I afford you?" What she says to the butler is a good indication of how she'll react to an unexpected situation.)

By now you see why we call this the Dream Garden. What you're doing is describing a dream, and asking people to put themselves into it. Their answers tell you more about them than you'd find out in a long weekend to Las Vegas. My friend, Al, tells me he tried this once during a convention, with a blonde in the bar of the Disneyland Hotel. "Tell me what your dream garden would look like?" asked Al. "I'm sitting in it," she answered sweetly, and ordered another martini—"stirred, not shaken, and very dry." Al never did get to question No. 2.

Doodlefreuds

Set this next trap for your friends by passing out pencils and sheets of paper with the following diagrams sketched out:

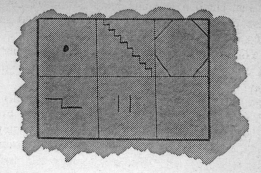

Give them only the most fragmentary instructions: "Do whatever you want to with these pictures."

Then, after the people have foolishly committed themselves, you can hang out a little sign saying, "The Doctor is IN"—and proceed to explain what the diagrams represent:

1. ego; 2. conformity; 3. sociability; 4. mechanical ability; 5. sexual drive, and 6. imagination.

I'll explain the interpretations. But first, for an example, let's look at the doodles drawn by my wife's cousin from Scranton, Pa.

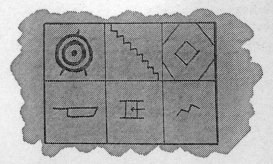

Here's how the interpretations go for each box:

1. A player who uses the dot as the center of his diagram is showing that he (or she) is self-centered, as did my wife's cousin. A less self-centered person might make the spot part of a bigger design—one of the wheels of a car, or the eye of a fish, perhaps.

2. Conformists always turn the stair-like design into—what else?—stairs. What would a nonconformist turn it into? A checkerboard, or maybe an accordion.

3. Sociability is demonstrated here by whether the player joins the lines together or not. The square doughnut design made here shows me a non-sociable type. A big mingler might connect it into something like the crossed Band aids made by a salesman I know:

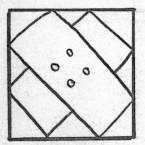

4. Mechanical ability shows in what the player makes out of the zigzag line. A nonmechanical type (above) makes it into a simple pot. I've seen people make it into a car fender, an airplane tail, or a boat.

5. Sexual drive is demonstrated by the number of times a player connects the two vertical lines together. The belt arrangement has two. One of the most interesting young ladies I've met recently made it a ball of string:

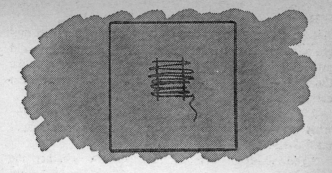

6. Imagination is demonstrated by how creative a design the player puts into the blank space, and by how well the space is used. Now a bird is a nice thought. But it doesn't fill much space. Wouldn't it have showed more imagination to have made a whole flock?

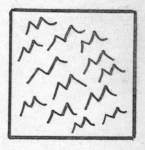

You'll probably say I'm being pretty dogmatic about these interpretations. Right! You've got to be firm with your patients—or they might gang up on you and make you do one, so they can all gleefully psychoanalyze you.

What's It Worth To You?

Now let's all have one on the house (my house) and go on to another conversational gambit: What's It Worth To You?

What's it worth to you, you ask, to have a toe chopped off? Surgically and neatly, of course. Would you give up a toe for $1,000? Then what about $10,000? What about $100,000 and a lifelong annuity for the children? Or maybe a Chris-Craft and mansion in Miami Beach, with all the taxes paid? Keep it up and you'll find that almost everyone has a price for a toe.

Then, with a crafty smile, you shift it to matters of morals—from giving up a toe to giving up a weekend. Suppose, you propose to a young woman, this filthy rich but disgusting old man (can you think of one?) offers you $1,000 to spend the weekend with him in the Poconos? Of course, she wouldn't. What about $10,000? Or $100,000? And maybe on the Riviera instead? With iron-clad guarantees that no one could ever find out?

Since it's all hypothetical, feel free to offer anything. The sky is the limit. There's bound to be some offer she can't refuse. Since the results are a foregone conclusion, the fun—and the interesting insights—come in the haggling over the price.

Who's To Blame?

This last story is for that time of the evening when the fire has burned down low, and everyone is in a mellow, friendly mood. I wouldn't advise using it after the psych-ins—people might be suspicious and give rigged answers. Save it for your friends when their defenses are down. It goes like this:

Seeking security and luxury, a beautiful young woman married an elderly but wealthy Cincinnati man. When she

94

started spending long hours at a riding stable across the Ohio River in Covington, Kentucky, he wasn't a bit suspicious; he trusted her completely. Meanwhile, she fell in love with the handsome young sportsman who owned the stable.

One day, despite a terrible rain, she said she was going riding and her husband believed her. But late that afternoon, when she got to the toll bridge over the Ohio, she was told that the bridge was going to soon be closed, because of the rising river—and she didn't have a dollar to pay the toll.

She pleaded with the bridge tender to let her cross free; she'd give him $10, $20—whatever he wanted—next time. He refused. "Rules are rules," he said, inflexibly. She hurried back to the stable and asked her lover for a dollar. "I can't give it to you," he said. "Our relationship could be entirely changed if I gave you money, even one dollar." He urged her to spend the night there and make up an excuse for her husband later, but she refused to do so—because, she said, her husband trusted her and expected her to return home that night.

So she returned to the river, attempted to cross on a railroad trestle, and was killed when high waters washed her car into the river.

That's the story. Here's the question your listeners must answer: Who caused this young woman's death? Her husband? Her lover? The guard at the bridge? Or did she bring it on herself?

After they give their answers, you explain that there isn't any answer. The theories people offer tell us answers about what sort of person THEY are—it's one of those stories that stirs people into giving answers that describe themselves.

Try it yourself, and see. Your uncle, the used car salesman, will probably say that the guy at the bridge should've taken the promise of $20 next time. A girl who's been around the block a few times might say—she should've stayed with the boyfriend and made up a story later. A youngster with overpermissive parents might easily blame the husband for being too trusting. People have a way of seeing themselves in this story—and, sometimes, the person in it who is like them sometimes turns out to be the one they blame.

... Who do *I* blame? Oh, I'm not in this story at all. What I'd like to know is, why didn't she borrow a dollar from the bartender? Oh, that's right, Bill. You're not in this story, either ...

Magic Made Easy
Or
Sleight Hand For
Every Man

. . . Now, see this martini? It's filled right up to the brim. You think you can get an olive into it? Try it. Ooops! Hand me a bar towel, will you, Bill? Now, let me show you how it's done.

Give me a new glass, eh, Bill? Now, the first thing I do is dry it thoroughly. We fill it right up to the top again, making sure the lip doesn't get wet. Now I drop the olive in, plip! And look: not a drop spills. Want to see me get another in? There. One more? Look—the martini is bulging out of the glass. And still not a thing drips. Know what holds the liquid in? Surface tension. Keep the brim dry—if there's a drop of water on it, your trick will trickle away—and you can pour yourself a high-rise martini . . .

In the old days they called this sort of thing a parlor trick. Never one to waste my time hanging around parlors, I picked this one up a few years back at a bar off Fifth Avenue where the olives were so big they displaced half the room for gin. Talk about giant size—those olives came four in a bottle. Once, when my hand was steadier, I could get the world's fullest martini—and six olives.

There are a few other tricks I've learned over the years (did I ever tell you I once ran away from home and worked in a carnival?) I'll tell you about them. They aren't the kind of tricks where you need a lot of skill. Some of them are simple enough to work right here at Bill's place. Others you'll want to try in your own home, where they'll add a whole new dimension to an evening by the fireside. (There's another advantage . . . you can't get kicked out!)

Try This, Buster!

Want to impress a tough guy, without going to the trouble of unbuttoning your 10-button, double-breasted, peppermint stripe blazer, lifting up your 6 inch wide magenta tie, and showing him your judo Black Belt? Twist a paper napkin into a long, thin shape—and ask him to tear it in half.

A napkin assumes the strength of stout cord when it is tightly twisted, and it's practically impossible to tear. He won't (we hope!) be able to do it. But you can do it, aided by a little legerdemain (all right—cheating). While the big guy is trying to tear the napkin in two, you dip your fingers in a glass of water. Then, when you offer to do the trick, let your wet fingers dampen the paper napkin. Moistened a bit, it suddenly becomes a cinch to tear in half.

. . . Hey, Bill, let me have a piece of string. That's what I said, a piece of string! I've got a little trick I want to show my friend here. Come on, you old pack rat, I know what you've got back there. I've seen the kind of things people leave on this side of the bar. There's gotta be some string—along with that old Elk's tooth and the Willkie button. Thanks, Bill. Now, watch this . . .

Salty Yarn

You claim you can get an ice cube out of a glass of water with this little ol' measly piece of string—without using your hands on the cube, of course. (Texans are great at this one. They try to lassoo the ice.) When it's time to show how it's done, you just lay one end of the string across the top of the ice cube and then pour a patch of salt on it. It takes about a minute for the string to freeze to the cube, after which you lift it out. This will work with other drinks besides water, too. But did you ever try your Jack Daniels salted?

. . . What's that, Bill? You hear they're making skimmed vermouth for fat martini drinkers? Very funny.

Pick a Buck

Here's another bit of trickery which calls for only the sleightest of hands:

Tell your friends you can tell which of five one dollar bills is which just by touching it to your forehead (you know, where all those brain waves come from). Ask them to take down the number of one bill—the serial number is on the black side, you know—and guarantee you can pick it out of a hat when it and the other four are wadded up and dropped into the hat.

You do the wadding. And when you wad up the bill that's been selected, wad up a nickel inside of it. It'll make that one heavier than the others, so you can tell it from the other three.

When you hold it up to your forehead, the extra weight —and your brain waves—enable you to say: "This is it!" Then you unfold it, pulling it past your thumb as though you're straightening out the kinks—when, in reality, you're palming the nickel. Like this:

While they're checking the serial number to make sure you're right, drop the nickel down your sleeve, or into your pocket, or into your Scotch and soda, or wherever it is you hide hot nickels.

Bottle Balance

Inertia, the free friendly service which keeps so many

of Bill's customers pinned for hours to their barstools, will also enable you to demonstrate a couple of interesting tricks.

Turn an empty beer bottle upside down on top of a quarter, and then see if anyone can figure out how to get the quarter out from under the bottle without touching it in any way, and without knocking it over.

It's easy, when you know the secret. Put a table knife flat on the bar and snap the blade sharply under the mouth of the bottle. This will knock out the coin, while inertia keeps the bottle from tipping over. Like this:

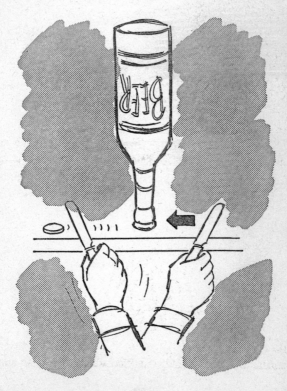

It's a Snap

Place a business card on the pad of the index finger of your left hand, and place a quarter on top of it, like this:

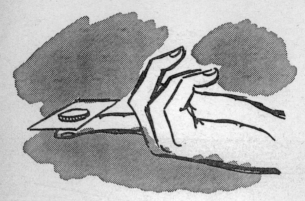

Here's what you're about to demonstrate: that you can remove the card with one move, without dislodging the coin.

Here's how:

With your other hand, using your thumb and middle finger the way a kid shoots marbles, snap the card quickly out from under the coin. If you're fast enough, and if you snap on the same plane as the card, the coin won't drop off on the floor.

(I saw my friend Al's first wife separate him from a secretary once much the same way. One moment Miss Murphy was sitting in his lap—then POW!—she was sitting in the chair, waiting for the pages of her dictation notebook to flutter down from the ceiling.)

Scratching for Change

Place two nickels on a table cloth, with a dime in

between. Put a glass upside down on top of the nickels so the dime is underneath the glass.

The idea is to get the dime out without removing the glass or touching the dime.

How it's done: scratch the table cloth on the outside of the glass. The dime will move toward the scratch. After a bit it will inch itself out from under the glass to where you can pick it up.

One thing, though—make sure there's a table cloth. You can tap on the top of a bar until the place closes and the dime won't budge. After the first hour or so, you'll probably get the impression that people are trying to avoid you.

The Shrunken Dollar

Knowing the appropriate tip is the mark of a gentleman. That applies when the service is terrible, too—when you might find one of Uncle Ed's Meager Gratuities well deserved.

Starting from a corner, crumple (don't fold) a dollar bill tightly and minutely into a small wad. Open it gently, so you don't pull the creases out. It'll look smaller. Do it again and it'll get even smaller. Keep crumpling. It'll give you something to do while waiting 20 minutes to get served another drink. After awhile it gets ridiculously small; eventually you can get it down to the size of a business card. It becomes just the thing for a modest tip —for modest service.

The Sunken Half

Order a glass of beer, and into it drop 50 cents. Then moisten the rim, and cover it with a piece of paper—the slick kind, not the absorbent sort. This, believe it or not, will seal off the beer well enough so you can flip it upside down on the bar without the beer spilling. The tricky part comes next: you carefully slip the paper out from underneath the lip of the glass.

What you have then is an upside down glass of beer sitting on the top of the bar with 50 cents gleaming up through the suds. Having left a tip, you then depart smartly from the premises—leaving the bartender to figure out how to retrieve his 50 cents without spilling the contents of the beer glass.

. . . I'd never try these on you, Bill. The service here is great. Now, let me see . . . if I've still got that Confederate C-note, I'll leave a generous tip, and be on my way.

Where There's Smoke . . .

You're having dinner with your wife or sweetheart (either one will do) at that charming little restaurant you're both so fond of—all atmosphere and candlelight. There's a glow in the air. Over an after-dinner brandy, you ask her—whoever she is—to blow out the candle. Then, as the smoke rises up from the wick, hold a lighted match about four inches above the candle—and the flame will run back down the smoke and re-light the candle!

A nice touch and just a little spectacular. When you do it, don't be surprised if she gives you her special, slow, sweet mysterious smile.

Making an Ash of Your Friend

With this trick you make an ash mark mysteriously jump from someone's right hand to his left. Before starting, you secretly dip the middle finger of your right hand into an ash tray so you get a heavy smudge of ashes on your finger.

Now tell a friend that you're going to try an experiment. But, since he's been drinking—at least he will have been at my house—he has to first extend his hands in front of him, palms down, as a test of steadiness.

When he does, grab his hands with yours and lift, saying, "A little higher, please." As you do, you secretly smear ashes from your finger into the palm of his left hand.

Complimenting him on his steadiness, you begin the experiment: ask him to close his left hand and keep it still, while he turns his right hand palm up.

Then you pick up a pinch of ashes from the ash tray

and place it on his open palm. Then tell him to close this hand, too, and explain that you're going to make a portion of the ashes jump unseen into his closed hand.

Tap the back of his left hand and ask him to open it. He'll find, amazingly, that some of the ash mark has seemingly jumped into the other hand!

The Mighty Dollar

Can a dollar bill hold up a glass?

Place a couple of glasses a few inches apart, put a dollar bill across the top of them, and challenge your companion (or, for that matter, someone else's companion) to put another glass on top of the bill without it resting on the top of the other glasses. In other words, the third glass has to be supported just by the dollar.

Here's how it's done:

Accordion pleat the dollar bill the long way. With enough pleats the bill will be strong enough to hold up a glass.

The Mysterious Mobius

Al, who is in computers, borrowed about four feet of cash register tape from Bill, the barkeep, the other night and bet me he could prove to me that the tape had only one side.

I fell for it. You can prove the same thing to disbelievers, too, if you want to follow Al's instructions for making what he calls a Mobius Strip. (It was invented by Mobius, a 19th-century German mathematician who specialized in seeing only one side to all his problems.) All you need is a strip of paper about four feet long and some tape (or a stapler) to hook the ends together.

If you taped the ends together in a big loop, you'd end up with an endless belt. But turn one end of the strip over 180 degrees, and then tape the ends together, and you've got a Mobius—a sort of feeley optical illusion. A piece of paper with only one side? It looks like this:

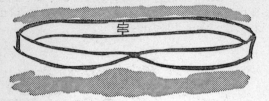

Want to prove it only has one side? Start drawing an arrow where the two ends of the tape were put together, and keep drawing it along the tape. When you get through, you'll have gone all the way around what seems like it should've been both sides, and come back to where you started—without lifting the pencil from the paper.

When Al finds someone who is unimpressed he asks them to carefully tear the Mobius down the middle and show him what the two pieces look like. That usually impresses them. Have your friends try it. It's impossible. (If you tear it in half it makes one long, mixed-up, groovy loop).

The Elevated Empty

Here are some slight sleights I can't recommend for impressing the British Ambassador, or a Harvard professor, but they're great when you want to show the kids one trick before you kick them out of the rumpus room so the party can really start.

Hold an empty quart-sized bottle mouth-down over the heater, or in the steam from boiling water, if there's a tea drinker around. "Want to see me lift this bottle without touching it?" you ask the kids. "Sure," they'll say, knowing anything (even this) is better than going to bed.

Then you turn the bottle upright and press a plate

sharply over its mouth, pressing the plate down tightly so no air can get in. Next you let it sit a moment or two so the air in the bottle can cool. (Coating the bottle lip with Greasy Kid Stuff, or even a touch of clam dip, will assure a better seal.) Then, when the air in the bottle is cool, lift up the plate. Like this:

The bottle will stick to the bottom of the plate and you can pick it up, just as you said you would, without touching it. How come? Heating the bottle expands air inside, and some rushes out. Sealing it off gives the air inside a chance to cool, and since there's less than there was before, you have a partial vacuum—which holds the bottle to the bottom of the plate.

Crockery Crookery

"More!" your appreciative audience will now cry, demanding an encore. (The younger they are and the closer it is to bedtime the more they will appreciate your legerdemain.) "Want to see me balance a cup on the point of a pencil?" you ask. (Of course they would.) "With the help of only a table fork and a winebottle cork?" (They damn well better agree, or there's no trick.)

Then you place the cork snugly in the handle of this cup, stick a fork into it around the cup handle, and, with the handle of the fork braced against the pencil, balance the teacup, just as you said, like this:

It's a real winner with the kindergarten set. But a word of warning: If the party's been going on too long, you might break quite a bit of crockery practicing before you get it done. And the farther you're in your cups, the harder it is to do.

If that won't send them to bed, give them another dime's worth.

The Talking Dime

"This dime," you say, "will tell us when it's time for you kids to hit the sack." How? "By going 'clink!'," you explain. "Let's put it here on this Coke bottle."

Unseen by your witnesses, you have slipped a little salt into the remnant of Coke left in the bottom of the bottle. A few drops of Coca-Cola and salt makes enough gas to cause the dime to bounce around for quite a length of time. As it does so, it clinks. Bedtime!

THE GENTLEMANLY
ART OF DRINKING

We've talked about the fun you can have while drinking. What about drinking itself?

It's about time someone said a kindly word about the magical products of fermentation——which have been much maligned, over the centuries, by those adamantly opposed to people having a little fun. Alcohol may well be man's best friend on earth——the dog is vastly overrated, except perhaps for the St. Bernard, who can make himself doubly endearing. Alcohol makes time pass pleasantly, eases crises, soothes broken hearts, makes battles easier to win or lose, and facilitates (as we all well know) a host of social events.

It's not really the villainous stuff some have termed it. Oh, it may make a villain more villainous, a weakling weaker, and a loudmouth louder. But it can also make a plain girl prettier, a nasty guy nicer, a good meal superb, and a pleasant evening a Night to Remember.

So come along with me, friends, and let's talk about man's second most favorite pastime. About where it started, and what it has become in these United States; about its names, myths, effects, aftereffects, and what the poets and sages have said about it before you and I were born—the gentlemanly art of drinking.

. . . Set 'em up, Bill. We've got a lot of old accounts to straighten out, and it's going to take all your skill and mine to get this story told. I'll make a deal with you. You make 'em, I'll drink 'em, and we'll get this job done. Oh, don't worry. I know the Irish have a reputation for being . . . well, shall we say, drinkers in quantity. But the Irish are a blessed race. It has been said that an Irishman is never totally drunk if he can reach out and grab a blade of grass to keep from falling off the face of the earth. Now, where was I going to start?

A Few Kind Words
About Man's Second
Favorite Pastime

There's a lot to be said for drinking—and a lot has been.

Like love, Drink has been praised in song and verse since the dawn of time, wine, rhyme and reason. Man through the ages has recorded the glories of

. . . the cup that clears
Today of past regrets and future fears.

The Bible contains many, many references to drinking —more urging us "to drink wine with a merry heart" than warning us against it. (There were more important things, then as now, to worry about.)

From the taverns of ancient Greece to the place downstairs and across the street, men have gathered to enjoy themselves and their leisure time. And, along the way, many have paused to admire the cup that brought them there—and have left behind a heritage of verse, some of which we now repeat, In Praise of Drinking.

"Give wine unto those that be of heavy heart."
(Prov. 31:6-7)

There are two reasons for drinking: one is, when you are thirsty, to cure it; the other, when you are not thirsty, to prevent it. Prevention is better than cure.

T.L. Peacock, *Melincourt*

The great should be as large in liquor as in love.

E.A. Robinson, *Ben Jonson*
Entertains Man From Stratford

The man that isn't jolly after drinking
  Is just a drivelling idiot, to my thinking.

Euripedes, *Cyclops*

Then trust me there's nothing like drinking
  So pleasant on this side the grave;
It keeps the unhappy from thinking,
  And makes e'en the valiant more brave.

Charles Dubin, *Nothin Like Grog*

Drink today, and drown all sorrow;
  You shall perhaps not do it tomorrow:
Best, while you have it, use your breath;
  There is no drinking after death.

John Fletcher, *The Bloody Brother*

I drink when I have occasion, and sometimes
  when I have no occasion.

Cervantes, *Don Quixote*

"In the fruit of the vine, therein lies healing
  for all mankind." *Koran*

If all be true that I do think,
There are five good reasons why we should
drink;
Good wine—a friend—or being dry—
Or lest we should be by and by
Or any other reason why

Henry Aldrich, *Reasons for Drinking*

My true feeling about respect for the ancient art of drinking is best explained by a Father's Day message run as a

118

public service advertisement a couple of years ago by the Seagram Distillers Company.

At the time I sent Seagram a letter complimenting them on it. I'm grateful that they have agreed to share their point of view with me in this barside book.

"When can I start to drink, Dad?"*

You knew it was coming. Sooner or later. And now you're going to have a little talk.

We can't give you the script. But we can give you our thinking.

Frankly, we view drinking as a grown-up pleasure. That means, flat out, that nobody tries to fudge the law. A young man waits to buy his first drink until he is legally permitted to do it.

But, even more important "grownup" means that he has arrived at a certain maturity. And just when that happens is a hard thing to judge.

We believe the tap root of balanced judgment has to be the parent. He defines what being adult means. By words. And by deeds.

If you see drinking as we see it—as a pleasure to be enjoyed sensibly, moderately, and in context with the rest of the good things of life—then, the chances are your son will too. The chances are he won't violate the trust you give him.

Certainly some young people do not always conduct themselves as they should. We would have our heads in the sand if we didn't see it. But that doesn't mean we have to go along with it.

For our part, we will continue to discourage this kind of behavior. We don't want that kind of business. And never have.

* Reprinted by permission of Seagram Distillers Company

119

You can help in a very positive way. Simply by expressing your own healthy, adult point of view. In what you say, and what you do. To your own son. And to the friends he may bring into your home.

Then, when the time comes, we can all be sure that the products we sell are in steady and responsible hands.

History of Alcohol
or
More Than You Need To Know About How It All Started

Fermentation

In the Beginning . . .

Man has been drinking as long as there has been alcohol, and alcohol first appeared on earth some two hundred million years ago, in what is called the late Paleozoic era. By that time, all the elements required for it to just naturally happen were already around. To explain how, I have to get a bit technical, but bear with me.

Simply stated, alcohol is produced from sugar (or from

a product which can be changed into sugar) by the process known as fermentation. Through the action of a chemical agent, yeast, certain changes take place in the sugar, resulting in both ethyl alcohol and carbon dioxide gas, with the gas escaping into the air. All wines are a result of this process. The yeast for wine is called saccharomycetes (how about that?), which form on the outside of ripening grapes. As the grapes are turned into juice, these saccharomycetes go to work—fermenting like crazy—and turn grape juice into wine.*

So there were these luscious grapes bursting on the vine, turning themselves into wine, and the Paleozoic man took a taste and liked what he tasted. Liked it a lot, as a matter of fact, according to the best scientific evidence. Later on, of course, man learned to control fermentation, but in the beginning the boys took it as they got it, which was plenty.

Another name for the Paleozoic era, by the way, is the Old Stone Age. Now I know why.

Liquid Bread

> How easy can the barley-bree
> > Cement the quarrel!
> It's aye the cheapest lawyer's fee
> > To taste the barrel.
> > > ROBERT BURNS

Beer, too, is a product of fermentation—from practically any cereal, but primarily barley—with an additional step: brewing. It goes back to the beginning of recorded history. Two Babylonian clay tablets, about six thousand years old, show men at work over a brewing vat and

---

* This explanation has been validated by Professor Irwin Corey, the world's foremost authority. If there are any questions, please address them to him.

give a very detailed recipe for brewing beer. (In their cups, they were inclined to Babylon.) About the same time, the Chinese recorded that the making of beer was decreed by heaven! Brewing, in fact, developed independently among several, separate agricultural peoples, just as baking, a similar process, did. It has even been referred to as "liquid bread."

The brewing process, itself, is a little too complicated for me to go into here, but it's a fascinating one and there's no better place to see it than at your favorite local brewery. (Mine happens to be Budweiser, which should surprise absolutely nobody.)

A word or two on how best to enjoy your favorite brew. For one thing, don't wash your beer glass with soap or soapy water. The soap leaves a fatty film on the inner surface of the glass breaking down the desired collar of foam. Use non-soapy detergents and always rinse the glass well with plain cold water. Further, the beer,

123

itself, should be poured straight down the middle of the glass so as to produce a nice head of foam, which locks in all that lovely flavor and aroma. (When I was in college, it was very much the thing to pour beer down the side of the glass in order to avoid a head of foam. But we were younger then and what did we know?) Finally, the best temperature at which to enjoy your beer is a cool and constant 40 degrees. Too cold and it will be flat and cloudy. Too warm, and the gas will break away from the liquid; you will get too much gas—which no one, in his right mind, ever really wants.

You like yours at 50 degrees? Let's not fight about it. Join me in another and remember what Bobby Burns said. How easy, indeed, "can the barley-bree cement the quarrel!"

Distillation

We've talked of wine and beer, products essentially of fermentation. But the process known as distillation provided man with an opportunity to expand his base of operation, so to speak. It provided him with "spirits"— the distilled essences of those potables* which he had enjoyed previously only in their fermented state.

Distillation, briefly, is based on the following. While the boiling point of water is 212°F., that of alcohol is 176°F. Thus, if heat is applied to an alcohol-containing liquid and the temperature is kept below 212°, all of the alcoholic vapors will be separated from the original liquid. If, at the same time, an apparatus is used (does the name "still" have a familiar ring?) whereby the alcoholic vapors are gathered and not allowed to escape into the air,

---

* I love that word. Potable. It sounds like something W. C. Fields might have said. It rhymes with tote-able and means "suitable for drinking."

it is possible to recondense them into liquid form. The result will be an alcohol of the highest purity.

Basically, it's just that simple. And, indeed, the apparatus used for distilling most spirits is still much the same as the one used by the original distillers, many centuries ago.

Although the source of distillation goes back to the ancient Egyptians, its modern history dates back to around 800 AD, when an Arabian alchemist named Jabir ibn Hayyan formulated the process.

It wasn't until the end of the thirteenth century, however, that a professor of medicine at the University of Montpellier, Arnaldus de Villanova, first saw its practical value. Dig the affectionate way he wrote about it in announcing his discovery:

"Limpid and well-flavored red or white wine is to be digested twenty days in a closed vessel, by heat, and then to be distilled in a sand bath with a very gentle fire. The true water of life will come over in precious drops, which, being rectified by three or four successive distillations, will afford the wonderful quintessence of wine. We call it aqua vitae, and this name is remarkably suitable, since it is really a water of immortality. It prolongs life, clears away ill-humors, revives the heart, and maintains youth."

And that, my children, is how brandy was born . . .

Brandy

It wasn't until the sixteenth century that brandy, the distilled essence of wine, was manufactured commercially, and that came about almost accidentally, out of an economic necessity. At that time there was a brisk trade in wine between France and Holland, all of which was carried on by sea. Casks of wine take up a lot of space. One day, as the story goes, a singularly enterprising

Dutch sea captain said to himself, "Why don't I eliminate the water from my wine, carry the basic stuff, and then when I get to Holland, I can just put the water back in? Think of all the space I'll save!" And so he did. But when he got to shore, several of his friends sampled his "concentrated wine" and shouted joyfully the equivalent of, "Forget about the water, baby. This is groovy."

Another splendid example of man's unquenchable ingenuity.

The Dutch, by the way, called the new product brandewijn (burnt wine), based on the heat or fire used in the distillation process. In time, the word became anglicized to what we know it as today.

Doctor, Doctor

Talking about human ingenuity, in the seventeenth century a Dutch physician named Doctor Sylvius decided to combine the juniper berry, which had exceptional therapeutic properties, with the essence of beer. The resultant distillate, he felt, would provide an inexpensive and readily available medicine. It did. Before long, all Holland was suffering from the ills that only the good doctor's medicine could cure. He called it *Genievre*, the French name for the juniper berry. The Dutch called it *genever* and the English first changed it to "geneva" and then shortened it to its present and practically universal name: gin.

Think of it. Every time you have a martini, you're really making yourself well.

Uisgebaugh-Uisgebaugh
(Celtic for Water of Life)

After distillation was discovered, it followed as the

night the day that man would go with what he had: if grapes were plentiful, he made brandy; where there was an abundance of grain, whiskey was distilled.

Though gin was popularly assumed to be the first liquor to be distilled from grain ("the first to come to the receptive attention of the civilized world," as the well-known authority, Berton Roueche, has smartly stated), it actually was preceded, as early as the late fifteenth century, by whiskey, flowing plentifully from the Scottish highlands and the florious Emerald Isle. (The Scots spell it whisky. The Canadians use the Scottish spelling; the Americans use the Irish spelling). It goes back even further, according to Irish legend, which counts it among the many good works—some say the best work—of St. Patrick. (Not many people believe that, but I do. I had an uncle, once, who was a leprechaun, and he told me . . .)

There are five main processes in the making of Scotch whisky, which is obtained primarily from barley: malting, mashing, fermenting distilling, and maturing and blending.* For a long while—well into the nineteenth century, in fact—there was considerable resistance outside of Scotland to Scotch Whisky ("My father," Sir Winston Churchill wrote in a memoir, "could never have drunk whiskey except when shooting on a moor or in some very dull chilly place"). The reason was its taste. In the making of pure Scotch, the malt barley is heated in peat-fired kilns. The peat gives off a pungent odor, giving the liquor a very dense, smokey flavor. Too dense and too smokey, in fact, for all but the most devoted connoisseurs.

But in 1860, a man named Andrew Usher—a grain whiskey distiller who also handled, as a sideline, a malt whiskey distillery—did something no one had ever thought of before: he blended the two together. It is the blended

* For a concise breakdown on the making of Scotch whisky, see Grossman's Guide to Wines, Spirits, and Beers.

Scotch (blending is done when the whiskies are from three to four years old) that most Scotch drinkers enjoy today.

Let's hear it for Andrew Usher!

Little Water

The Russians, too, have been known to make a distilled spirit from time to time. In fact, they originated one of them. Perhaps you've heard of it: vodka.

It is generally assumed that vodka is made only from potatoes, but that is not entirely correct. It is also made from various grains, principally corn with some wheat added. Another misconception: that the Russians drink vodka of a very potent proof. Not so. Vodka is generally marketed in Russia, Poland and the Baltic countries at only 80 proof (which makes a little easier to believe all those stories about Russians downing glass after glass of the stuff at various state functions and other joyous occasions).

Vodka means "little water," which is a nice way of putting it, if you stop and think about it. Affectionate. Gentle.

I like their attitude. Maybe we will get along with them some day.

America, America

What was happening in our own land while Europeans were lapping up all that aqua vitae? Were the natives idle? We know they were restless.

The making of whiskey in this country was introduced by Scottish-Irish settlers, who arrived here in considerable numbers after the Revolution. To these good people, the making of whiskey was practically a natural phase of farming. Along the coastal plain rye was plentiful, and the drink took it for its source, flavor and name. In Appalachia, where the grain was corn, whiskey was corn (or sour mash) whiskey. Aged properly, it became known as Bourbon. Ever hear of the Rev. Elijah Craig? He ranks with Edison, Bell and the Brothers Wright, and he's practically an unknown. He was living in Georgetown, Ky., in the fall of 1789, when he made his great invention. You may guess what it is when I tell you George-town is in Bourbon County.

Yep, the Rev. Mr. Craig, a Baptist clergyman, was the inventor of what came to be known as Kentucky Bourbon. The art of whiskey making was brought to America by the Scotch-Irish settlers of the hill country. The good reverend found a way of making it from sour mash corn. It wasn't moonshine, either. He was the one who discovered that whiskey stored in charred oak barrels acquires a more pleasing taste.

By 1810 the state was turning out two million gallons of bourbon a year. In Maryland and Pennsylvania, where there was more rye than corn, they turned out a slightly different product. What do you think they called it?

By 1900—with the application of the Scottish principle of blending to Kentucky bourbon and Pennsylvania rye—all the forms of distilled liquor now known had been discovered.

Amen.

Drinking in America

or

Documents of

(Happily) Yesteryear

"Land!" cried the lookout on the Santa Maria. "I'll drink to that!" said Columbus. It was the beginning of drinking in America.

In a Tavern

You may not find it in the history books, but there's a lot more about drinking that is. Take taverns, for instance. Ever consider their contribution to American history? The early Americans found it convenient to be patriotic in a convivial setting. Look at the names of a few historic taverns:

Montagne's Tavern—On Lower Broadway in New York, it was the headquarters of the Sons of Liberty. Revolution was hatched here.

Buckman's Tavern—This is where the patriots assembled as the British troops were marching on Lexington, Mass., early April 19, 1775. "The British are coming!" cried Paul Revere. "We've just got a minute," said one of the patriots, and most of them disappeared into Buckman's. They've been known since as the Minute Men. (As it turned out, they had several hours, and we presume they spent it wisely. What other preparation can you make for a long war?)

City Tavern—The Philadelphia hostelry where the

First Continental Congress met. It had the first smoke-filled rooms in American politics.

Fraunce's Tavern—Where the Vigilance Committee of New York gathered to keep an eye on the British, this being prior to the advent of televised football. Its owner later spied on the Redcoats for George Washington, and it was at Fraunces' that Washington said farewell to his officers after victory in 1783.

The Indian Queen Tavern—In Philadelphia, where Thomas Jefferson framed his first draft of the Declaration of Independence.

The Fountain Inn—In Baltimore, was where Francis Scott Key completed the "Star Spangled Banner." (The music, fortunately for the other guests, was added later.)

The tavern was a traditional American meeting place. So was the church. The fact that more history was made in taverns than in churches was probably because taverns had fireplaces. Or something.

Did you know that Martin Van Buren, our eighth President, was born in a tavern—his father's? Or that Abraham Lincoln was a part owner of a tavern in New

132

Salem, Illinois, in 1833? This promising career was ruined when he was elected to the Illinois Legislature the next year.

Do It Yourself

In the earliest days the public houses stocked American-made beer, wine, ale and cider, favoring local products because of the high cost of shipping goods (and glugs) from England. (Rum—the distillate from the fermented juice of sugar cane, sugar cane molasses, or other sugar cane by-products, was being made from molasses in the West Indies, and some of it was imported.) An anonymous 17th century manuscript entitled, "A Brief Description of the Island of Barbadoes" contains perhaps the earliest surviving reference to its name and origins. "The chief fuddlings* they make on the island," the author states, "is rum-bullion, alias kill-devil—a hot, hellish and terrible liquor." Then, some enterprising New Englanders thought: why not bring the molasses here and we'll make our own rum?

They did, too—and the history of the continent was changed.

New England began making more rum than the colonies could drink. The colonials owed England for manufactured goods, and, not being able to bank rum, the English wanted gold. In Africa, rum was as good as money. Rum could be swapped there for slaves.

So the entrepreneurs and ship owners worked it out this way:

—Molasses was brought from the West Indies to New England and turned into rum.

—The rum was shipped to Africa and traded for slaves.

—The slaves were brought to the American south and

---

* Fuddling? Look that up in your Funk and Wagnalls.

sold for gold to plantation owners who needed them as field hands.

—And the gold was paid to the English merchants for the manufactured goods needed in the colonies.

The English tried to tax the importation of molasses into the colonies, the colonists began to mutter about "taxation without representation," the Sons of Liberty and the Vigilance Committee met to have a drink and talk this thing over, slaves poured into the south—and at least two wars—and a lot of rum—were brewing. There was nothing anyone could do to head it off. History, like in-laws, is something which just happens to you.

How The West Was Won

The West was being won, meanwhile, and it wasn't being won by a bunch of teetotalers, either.

Whiskey making, although done on a small scale, was done by almost everybody. It became a major industry along the frontier; bushels of grain, you see, were hard to carry; bottles of whiskey weren't. In 1791 the young United States government, scratching for funds, decided that a tax on the manufacture of whiskey would produce revenue. The farmers of the home-brew country reacted with the first protest march in U.S. history, except they carried Kentucky rifles instead of picket signs. It took 15,000 militia to settle the issue; the federal government could tax whatever it wanted to tax. Some farmers were adamant. Some began the country's first illegal stills. The rest moved farther west, into Indian Territory, escaping the revenuers, helping push the frontiers out into the plains, and, in general, making heroes of themselves.

We all know the part saloons played when the West finally got Out West. What was built first in every town? The saloon.

Can't you see the owner telling the carpenters: "And

134

make that railing up there kinda flimsy, boys, so the guy in the black hat can fall through easy and land on the far table when the guy in the white hat spots him in the mirror behind the bar."

Yes, a wet and wild old time was being had by all. Almost all. A few people—who didn't seem to realize that there'd be guys in black hats and guys in white hats whether they were in the saloon, in church, or down at the OK Corral—decided temperance was the thing. For everybody.

The Antis

It was way back in 1735 that the colony of Georgia tried the first prohibition. A law was passed halting the import of rum (this was before the Rev. Craig's historic discovery, you'll recall). It didn't work. How can a man chop down trees and shoot Indians all day and then relax in the evening with only a beer? The law was so widely broken, it was repealed in 1742.

There was a message here, but it was ignored.

By the 1800's the temperance movement was thriving. Do-gooders were better organized than tipplers, and a number of states went dry. Most such local-option laws were soon repealed. It wasn't hard for the temperance people to get the laws passed; it was human nature they couldn't change.

Saloons, where everybody, it was suspected, was having a heck of a good time, really infuriated the dries. The Anti-Saloon League was formed, and, in 1869, the Prohibition Party. And you know what it was they wanted prohibited.

In 1896, the New York State legislature—in a burst of prohibitionary zeal—passed a Liquor Tax law, one of the purposes of which was to close all saloons on Sunday. The law imposed severe punishment for anyone who passed stuff over the bar on the Sabbath day. It was called the Raines Law, after Sen. John Raines, author of the sponsoring bill.

An exception was made, however, in favor of hotels . . . as long as guests received their drinks together with food regularly and properly set out on the table.

What happened, of course, was inevitable: every saloon in New York became a hotel. The saloonkeeper set up a couple of cots and kept a false register behind the bar, and customers sat happily around a table on which was placed a "prop" sandwich.

If you ever really wanted to stay at the "hotel," there was usually one bedroom set aside for guests. In fact, some places had more than one bedroom. They had several bedrooms. But that's another story . . .

In 1900 a former school teacher named Carry Nation decided that her prayers and denunciations didn't seem to be closing the saloons very fast; when she'd shut up and listen she could still hear the clink of glasses inside those swinging doors. That's when she bought a hatchet.

She'd go busting in the door, swinging furiously, busting open kegs and smashing bottles—while strong men either moved out smartly or watched, helplessly, cowering in corners, with tears in their eyes. She called it a "hatcheta-tion;" today it'd most likely be known as an ax-in. You probably won't be surprised to find out that in 1901 her husband divorced her. She went down swinging, as they say in baseball, in 1911.

The Prohibition Party, meanwhile, was becoming a force in politics. They ran candidates for President, and, though they never came close, they amassed a lot of votes —enough in 1884 to swing New York State to Grover Cleveland. Politicians respected them. They were danger-ous. They soon showed just how dangerous . . .

During World War I the output of alcoholic beverages was limited as a part of the war effort (but we somehow won it, anyhow). The drys took advantage of this, and the preoccupation of a lot of busy fighting men, to wage a furious campaign in Congress. They intimidated politi-cians, while—out in the grassroots—orators like militantly anti-drink evangelist William (Billy) Sunday were stirring up emotions.

In 1917 Congress passed what was to become the 18th Amendment to the Constitution, and it was subsequently ratified by the legislatures of three-fourths of the states, as required by law, and became effective beginning in 1920. Mind you, it was never put to a popular vote. Want to know what it said?

Eighteenth Amendment
"SECTION 1. After one year from the ratification of this article the manufacture, sale, or transportation of intoxicating liquors within, the importation thereof into, or the exportation thereof from the United States and all territory subject to the jurisdiction thereof for beverage purposes is hereby prohibited. SECTION 2. The Congress and several states shall have concurrent power to enforce this article by appropriate legislation. SECTION 3. This

article shall be inoperative unless it shall have been ratified as an amendment to the Constitution by the legislatures of the several states, as provided in the Constitution, within seven years from the date of the submission hereof to the States by the Congress."

All that remained was to enforce it. A fellow you might never otherwise have heard of, Rep. Andrew Volstead of Minnesota, introduced what was to become the Volstead Act. It was passed in 1919 over the veto of President Woodrow Wilson.

It became the National Prohibition Act of 1920. Here's what it said:

Volstead Act

It defined intoxicating beverages as those containing over ½ of 1 per cent (0.5) alcohol by volume and "fit for beverage purposes." It forbade anyone to "manufacture, sell, barter, transport, import, export, deliver, furnish, or possess any intoxicating liquor" so defined . . . The Commissioner of Internal Revenue was charged with enforcing the Act, with powers to investigate offenders and report them to U.S. attorneys for prosecution. Penalties for violators were set at maximums of $1,000 or 6 months in jail or both for first offenders, and $10,000 or 5 years or both for second offenders. Places selling liquor illegally could be padlocked by court injunction for 1 year, and vehicles used for transport of liquor could be confiscated.

The drys were triumphant. Said Billy Sunday, a former

baseball player who was one of the great crowd pleasers on the Sawdust Trail:

"Men will walk upright, women will smile and children will laugh. Hell will be forever rent."

The Roaring Twenties

I'm afraid to say, after sober consideration, that if hell was rent, it was rent with loud, long laughs. Prohibition, called the Noble Experiment, didn't produce the expected golden era. It produced the Roaring Twenties.

The Volstead Act simply couldn't be enforced. Smuggling and illegal manufacture made it a laughing stock. People were going to drink and there weren't enough police in the world, much less in the United States, to stop it. And in a land where almost everyone violated the law and millions of dollars poured into illicit channels, new acts of lawlessness became the norm for American living.

The language changed as new words were coined to match the way of life: bathtub gin, bootlegger, speakeasy, rum runner. There was even a contest to think of the best word to describe the "lawless drinker." The winning word: Scofflaw.

Our fathers and grandfathers were drinking some of the worst booze seen since the days of Stone Age grape. Some people were blinded by it, and there's no telling how many stomachs were ruined. Think of the worst drink you ever had. Believe me, it would've tasted great in 1925.

Amid the general lawlessness, guys in big limousines with dark suits and fedoras pulled down over their eyes stepped in to argue over who was going to operate what had once been the wholesale liquor trade. Tommy guns blazed along the city streets, hoods went swimming (briefly) wearing cement overshoes, and St. Valentine's Day took on an entirely new meaning.

Gangsterdom, epitomized by Al Capone, thrived—slowed up only a little by Elliot Ness and his unreachable Untouchables. By 1928, an estimated $25 million a day was being paid out to the underworld to slake what must have been a record thirst. People were drinking who probably otherwise wouldn't have bothered. But, since it was fashionable to break the law, we became a nation of scofflaws. All in all, it was a bad time for this proud land.

Prohibition lasted a lot longer than I thought before I looked into it: 13 years, 10 months and 19 days, to be exact. Remember when the militia had to enforce the government's right to tax whiskey, back in 1791? Well, during Prohibition, the estimated tax loss was over $4 billion! Not much today, but in those days a billion was a real billion.

But the nation finally came to its senses. What was to become the 21st Amendment—Repeal—was passed by Congress in 1933. (In those days it was more important whether you were a wet or a dry than whether you were a Democrat or a Republican.) It was ratified by the required three-fourths of the states the same year. Here's how it read:

Twenty-First Amendment

"SECTION 1. The Eighteenth Article of Amendment to the Constitution of the United States is hereby repealed. SECTION 2. The transportation or importation into any State, Territory or possession of the United States for delivery or use therein of intoxicating liquors, in violation of the laws thereof, is prohibited. SECTION 3. This article shall be inoperative unless it shall have been ratified as an amendment to the Constitution by conventions in the several states, as provided in the Constitution within seven years from the date of submission hereof to the States by Congress."

Note that it said you still couldn't take alcoholic beverages anyplace "in violation of the laws thereof," and a number of states, counties and cities maintained full or partial prohibition under local option. Some do to this day. In none is the letter of the law scrupulously obeyed.

Happy Days Are Here Again

As suds flowed freely across the land, and gin came from the store instead of the bathtub, there were permanent side effects of the long dry spell. The underworld, by then firmly established, went into other enterprises of shady nature—bookmaking, the numbers game, gambling ships, floating crap games, pinball machines—and it is still with us, draining off illicit millions every day.

The Prohibition Party, having seen its Noble Experiment fail miserably, went into a decline, and has never been a political force since.

Shu Ching, a Chinese spokesman of 650 B.C., had said it a long, long time ago:

"Men will not do without beer. To prohibit it and secure total abstinence is beyond the power of the stages."

I'll drink to that!

The Drinking Man
or
.003 Isn't Much, But
It's A Start

I missed what must have been a smashing television program. Seems the English temperance people got BBC to let them demonstrate the evils of drink on live television. They set up a complicated driving test in front of the TV cameras and asked volunteer motorists to drive it once, cold sober, and a second time after they'd had a couple of belts of booze. The idea was to show how alcohol slows the reflexes, causes muscular discoordination, and ruins your driving skill.

That's what was supposed to happen, but it didn't work out that way. The volunteers got in their cars cold sober and proceeded to do the worst driving they'd ever done in their lives. Then, each had a couple of slugs of Scotch. Suddenly, they began to feel good all over! Smiling and confident, they got in their cars—and this time passed the test with, as they say in England, Flying Colours.*

The truth of the matter is, there are a lot of things we can do better after a drink or two. (I've got my list, you've got yours.) What does this stuff do for the drinking man, anyway? Let's take a look at what the experts say it does.

What It Does For You

—It relieves tension. It makes it easier for you to relax, and, if Things Go Better With Coke, believe us, they go even better with Coke with something in it. That's why drinking time is usually a time of conviviality.

—It increases your appetite, by encouraging the flow of digestive juices. That's why a drink before dinner makes you hungrier.

—It dilates your arteries. That's why geriatrics specialists recommend a drink for older people. It fights arteriosclerosis. There are those who say it definitely contributes to longevity. The last two Civil War veterans, ages 108 and 113, said they regularly took a nip.

---

* Studies have borne this out. A 1963 study of 15,000 drivers in Grand Rapids, Mich., by the Indiana University department of police administration, found that drivers with between .01 and .04% alcohol in their blood—the equivalent of one or two mild drinks—were less likely to cause accidents than nondrinkers.

All this wasn't just discovered recently. St. Paul gave Timothy the following advice in Ephesus:

"Drink no longer only water, but use a little wine for thy stomach's sake and thine infirmities."

Most doctors approve of moderate drinking, and almost all those I know admit they like a cocktail themselves. There are exceptions. A drinking man of my acquaintance was limited by his doctor to one drink a day; right now he's up to May 10, 1993. (I think he's also shopping around for a new doctor.)

My favorite physician of all time would have to be Hieronymus Brunschwig (that was his name, I swear it), the titan of 15th-century German medicine, surgery and pharmacology, who wrote:

"Aqua vitae (brandy) is commonly called the mistress of all medicines. It eases the diseases coming of cold. It comforts the heart. It heals all old and new sores on the head. It causes a good color in a person. It heals baldness and causes the hair well to grow, and kills lice and fleas. It cures lethargy. Cotton wet in the same and a little wrung out again and so put in the ears at night going to bed, and a little drink thereof, is of good against all deafness. It eases the pain in the teeth, and causes sweet breath. It heals the canker in the mouth, in the teeth, in the lips, and in the tongue. It causes the heavy tongue to become light and well-speaking. It heals the short breath. It causes good digestion and appetite for to eat, and takes away all belching. It draws the wind out of the body. It eases the yellow jaundice, the dropsy, the gout, the pain in the breasts when they be swollen, and heals all diseases in the bladder, and breaks the stone. It withdraws venom that has been taken in meat or in drink, when a little treacle is put thereto. It heals all shrunken sinews, and causes them to become soft and right. It heals the bites of a mad dog, and all stinking wounds, when they be washed therewith. It gives also young courage in a person, and causes him to have a good memory. It purifies the five wits of melancholy and of all uncleanness."

What It Does To You

You probably all know this, but it's worth repeating.

The absorption of alcohol into the blood stream begins practically the minute you start drinking. How quickly it is absorbed depends on several factors:

—the alcoholic content of the drink itself (the stronger the drink, the faster the rate of absorption)

—the kind of drink it is (wine and beer, for example—probably because they retain some of the solid materials from which they were made—are absorbed more slowly than, say, pure alcohol diluted to the same concentration)

—the nutritional state of the stomach at the time, perhaps the most important (the presence of other substances in the tummy slows down the rate of alcohol entering the bloodstream)

In other words, when you drink, whatever you're drinking—eat a little something!

The How Of It

Now, this next part sounds pretty technical, but read it carefully. It might be something to remember if a local constable wants you to blow up one of those balloons some night on the way home from the office Christmas party.

The amount of alcohol in your bloodstream is used as a legal measure of how drunk you are. All the while

146

you're putting alcohol into your blood, your liver, that organ of temperance, is trying desperately to sober you up —by keeping the alcohol out of your blood. (The normal alcohol to your bloodstream. If you drink faster than one start.) The trouble is, your liver can only handle about one ounce of alcohol an hour. That's about what's in one really stiff mixed drink, or a couple of weak ones.

In other words, you could drink one or two drinks an hour all night long and stay clinically and legally sober.

Each stiff drink is going to contribute about .025 of alcohol to your blood stream. If you drink faster than one good one an hour, those .025s are going to start accumulating in there. In most states you're considered legally drunk when your blood gets up to .15. Let's say you stop by the local innkeeper's after work and start adding to that .003:

6 p.m.	.025
6:15	.025
6:30	.050 (somebody bought you double)
6:45	.025
7:00	.025
plus	.003 to begin with
	.153 (you're in trouble!)

But what about old Lily Liver, the temperance worker? Between 6 and 7 she's been able to get rid of .025, right? So you're back at .128. And, if you've eaten a lot of hors d'oeuvres—well, you just might make it home sober. Not sober as a judge, but sober enough to meet one.

Thinking about stopping for coffee on the way home? Forget it, pal Coffee can't do a thing for you. Pour coffee into a drunk and all you get is a wide-awake drunk! Your best bet is to get home before the .025s start adding up.

This is the way a student of conviviality, Emil Bogen, figured it all out:

If a person has less than 0.05 per cent alcohol concentration in the blood, that person is apt to be *dull* and *dignified*.

If the concentration of alcohol is between 0.05 and 0.10 per cent, the individual, if a gentleman, is apt to be *dashing* and *debonair,* while if a lady, she may well be *delightful* and *desirable*.

If the concentration of alcohol rises in a person to a level between 0.1 and 0.2 per cent, the person is often *daring* and *devilish*.

If the concentration reaches between 0.2 and 0.3 per cent, the person may become *dangerous* and *disheveled*.

If it is around 0.4 per cent, the individual is *delirious* and *disgusting*.

If it reaches 0.5 per cent, the person is *clearly drunk*.

If it reaches 0.6 per cent, the person is *dead drunk*.

What about people who go from *dull* and *dignified*—and, after just a few belts—proceed directly to *delirious* and *devilish?* Let them heed the advice given by the English poet George Herbert, circa 1625:

Drink not the third glass—
Which thou cans't not tame once it is within thee.

W. C. Fields

or

The Drinking Man's
Drinking Man

No book on the drinking arts would be complete without mention of the man who is my favorite drinking man of all time: W.C. Fields, alias Charles Bogle, Mahatma Kane Jeeves, Otis Criblecoblis, Elmer Nesselrode, Larson E. Whipsnade, Ampico J. Steinway, A. Pismo Clam and Egbert Souse ("Pronounced with the accent on the final E, my good man").

He used to work on the movie set with a chilled container of what he referred to as "pineapple juice." For pineapple juice, it had a very strange odor—almost like gin, with perhaps a hint of vermouth. Returning to his chair one day after a close-up, he took a swig—and almost exploded.

"Godfrey Daniel and Mother of Pearl," he bellowed. "Some sidewinder has put pineapple juice in my pineapple juice!"

When he played golf he always secreted a dozen whiskey miniatures in the pockets of his golf bags before setting out for an afternoon on the links. "I always keep a supply of stimulants handy in case I see a snake," he said, "which I also keep handy."

The fact that many of his best movie scenes took place in bars and pool halls was attributed by some to the fact that he had more than a passing familiarity with such premises. When he was a boy of 11 in Philadelphia, he belted his father in the chops and ran away from home— and spent his nights sleeping on poolroom floors and in barroom cellars. (That bulbous nose, by the way, was the product of street fights, not strong drink; it was old scar tissue, not dry martinis, which gave it that heroic dimension.) He knew he wanted to go into show business, but he didn't have a musical instrument. But a light-fingered, clever young chap could get his hands on a simpler sort of prop. He was soon one of the best 7-ball jugglers on the vaudeville circuits. Later he began adding asides of his own, and it wasn't too long before they became the most important part of his routine.

Finally he dropped the balls—on purpose—and made his way on his wry humor and his impersonation of the world's greatest con man. There were those who said it was type casting.

He was one of the few comedians who was as funny off the screen as on it. His friends recorded lines like:

In the hospital: "Bring me a sedative—with an olive in it."

On his youth: "I never drank a thing stronger than beer until I was 12."

And "It was a woman who drove me to drink—and, you know, I never even wrote to thank her."

On the set (After he had spiked Baby Leroy's milk with gin, and he fell asleep): "Send him home. The kid's no trouper."

Refusing a dinner invitation: "Sorry, I never eat on an empty stomach."

On travels: "Crossing the Andes I lost my corkscrew —and had to live on food and water for a week."

On strong drink: "I always know when I've had enough —when my knees start bending backward."

Or: "Myself, I'm a reformed teetotaler."

152

Remember him in "The Bank Dick" (1940)? Collectors of Fieldsiana can tell you it took place in Lompoc, California, (pronounced, then as now, Lom poke) and that the bank examiner was J. Pinkerton Snoopington. Do you remember how he thwarted him? He took him into the Black Pussycat Cafe and asked his friend, the bartender:

"Has Michael Finn been here today?"

Fields died early Christmas morning, in 1946, in the unlikely city of Pasadena, California—which has a reputation for being bigger than Lompoc, but a lot quieter. Before he slipped into his last coma, he awakened to see the room crowded with doctors and nurses. They had always been his enemies. (In one film he had Dr. Stall listen to the patient's heart and then prescribe: "Cut out all health foods! That'll be $10. The nurse will return your shirt with your receipt!")

He motioned his secretary to his bedside, put a finger to his lips—and winked. Then he closed his eyes for the last time.

Definitions for the
Drinking Man
or
Words to Wet Your
Whistle By

There are a few basic things every drinker should know about drinking, and, for those whose education has been sadly neglected, let me give you a few definitions. There are whole dictionaries of words about alcohol, so to simplify things, I'm just going to tell you about the things I think are interesting.

I mention a few specific drinks, mostly because I like them, and what goes into them. But just a few. If you want a recipe book, buy a recipe book.

Now and then a few of my prejudices may slip in, so don't be surprised if you get into an argument following your Uncle Ed's advice. Some people get furious with me, too, because I'm right all the time.

ABSINTHE—A mixture of herbs, spices, and other aromatic flavorings, among them, wormwood—whose herbiage is so potent it makes a good moth killer. Taken over a period of time, absinthe affects the nerve centers and produces hallucinations, delirium and idiocy. It was outlawed in France in 1908 after authorities found a lot of the local wine seller's favorite customers had begun to babble before they had anything to drink. The United States barred its import in 1912. As with most other things which are illegal, it can still be had. It is emerald green. Not recommended.

ALCOHOL—Curious about the origin of the word "alcohol" itself? I was surprised to discover it is of Arabic derivation. There is some question as to whether it stems from "alkhul," meaning essence, or from "alghul," meaning ghost or evil spirit.

BROWN BAG LAW—In some states you can't buy a drink across the counter, or at a table, but the law says you can bring your own bottle. What do you carry it in? A brown bag. The dining room provides what's called a set up—the glasses and the mix. A librarian friend of mine told me he went into a Georgia restaurant once with a bag containing a pint bottle of rubber cement, and the waiter brought him a Coke and a glass full of ice before he could explain. (It made a terrible drink, he said, but it did seem to improve the food.)

COCKTAIL—It is reputed that the name cocktail originated in a tavern near New York around 1788. When American and French army officers came to the tavern known as "Betsy's Tavern," Betsy, the barmaid, would serve them a concoction of mixed spirits called "bracers."

Often the officers would tease the barmaid about the plump, juicy chickens owned by a Tory neighbor. (I don't understand what they teased her about, but that's how the story goes.) She threatened to make them eat their words.

One day they were served a chicken feast. When the officers had eaten their fill, and stepped to the bar, they found each glass of bracers decorated with a cock's tail from the Tory rooster. One Frenchman laughed, lifted his glass, and said, "Vive le cocktail!" From then on, bracers were called cocktails.

What a strange story.

HIGHBALL—A tall (or, in some bars, not very damn tall) glass of iced and diluted spirits; in other words, something you put mix in. Some examples: bourbon and water (in the South and Southwest, they call it branchwater, the same thing by another name), Scotch and soda, rum and Coke, gin and tonic. Bourbon and Coke can be mixed, but not drunk; Scotch and Coke can't even be poured into the same glass. At least not while I'm watching. A highball, unlike a cocktail, can be drunk anytime —before or after dinner, as a midnight snack, with one's breakfast cornflakes, anytime.

HORSE'S NECK—A non-alcoholic drink ordered by someone on the water wagon. (This keeps me from having to define water wagon—ridden by someone who drinks Horse's Necks.) Kiddie versions are called a Shirley Temple or a Davy Crockett.

MANHATTAN—Next to the martini, this is the nation's best beloved cocktail. It is served in one of those shallow, stemmed glasses, like a martini, somewhat less rarely in a short, fat (lowball) glass on the rocks (that's ice, WTCU spies, that's ice). It is made usually from bourbon and sweet vermouth at about 3-1. A perfect Manhattan refers not to the way it's stirred but to the ingredients: it is made with dry vermouth, or, sometimes, a bit of each. A Scotch Manhattan is called a Rob Roy, and you can ask for a perfect Rob Roy, too.

MARTINI—America's favorite cocktail. The run-of-the-ginmill martini is about 4-to-1 gin to dry vermouth, but it can be made as dry as 15-to-1. Normally, it calls for an olive, but it can also come with an onion, becoming a Gibson, or with just a twist of lemon. (I saw one purist who refused even the twist of lemon; he stormed to his feet and told the bartender: "If I'd wanted lemonade, I'd've ordered lemonade!") Usually a martini is stirred and strained into a shallow glass—the classic "standing up" martini—but it can also be poured over ice—"on the rocks." Some claim it can be made with vodka, but it isn't quite the same. As you can see, the subject is so complicated I'll have to write a whole chapter on martinis.

MICKEY FINN—A knockout of a cocktail, devised by a Chicago barkeep at the turn of the century and named for him. Mickey put knockout drops in customers' drinks so they'd pass out and cohorts would rob them. (It was apparently chloral hydrate.) Mickey's place was noted for its stunning service!

PROOF—A measure of the alcoholic content of a beverage. In 17th century England they mixed gunpowder with the beverage and then tried to set it on fire; it would burn only when the alcoholic liquid was sufficiently free of water to permit it. If it burned this, then, was the proof of alcohol. England and the United States now use different ways of measuring proof—an alcoholmeter or a hydrometer— and, for some reason, use different scales. In the United States a 100-proof drink is 50% alcohol; in Britain it is 57% alcohol by volume. So a 100-proof jolt in England is stronger than one here; this is why they call it Merrie England.

SAKE—Called a rice wine and named for the Japanese city of Osaka, it is really a beer—since it is made from a grain instead of a grape. Alcoholic content is 14 to 17%. It is served warm.

SPEAKEASY—Named for the soft voice with which customers made themselves known ("Psst! Harry sent me!"), they were the illicit saloons of the Prohibition era. It takes a real oldtimer to know that the term pre-dated Prohibition; the name was first applied to saloons operating without licenses in 1889, in New York City.

TEETOTALER—A total abstainer. The word is believed to be of English origin. One account says it came from a stammering temperance worker from Lancashire named Richard Turner, who used to demand "tee-tee-total abstinence" of his listeners.

TOAST—The term "toast" is said to have originated in Bath, England, around 1650. At this time there was in vogue a peculiar English habit: drinkers sometimes floated bits of toast in their drinks, the way we sometimes put crackers in soup.

The story goes that a famous beauty was in the public baths for which Bath was known. An admirer filled his glass with her bath water—famous for its salubrious qualities—and said, "To your health!" to the lovely creature. And, forthwith, drank it off.

"I wouldn't care for your drink," said a companion, "but I'd certainly like the toast in it."

I'm not sure I understand this story. Or the one about the word "cocktail" either, for that matter.

TOM AND JERRY—a highly spiced punch. The name derives from Egan's Life in London, sub-titled: Days and Nights of Jerry Hawthorne and his Elegant Friend Corinthian Tom (1828).

VERMOUTH—An aromatic wine which has been around since the days of ancient Greece. It is made with herbs, roots, leaves, plants, peelings, seeds and, sometimes, a few flowers and a touch of wormwood. That's where the name came from— say wermut, the German word for vermouth, with a mouth full of sauerkraut, and it comes out something like vermouth.

It was first used as a flavoring to cover up the taste of bad wine. Now it comes in two attractive colors: green (dry vermouth, used in martinis) and red (sweet vermouth, used in Manhattans). Sometimes they are called French and Italian, respectively, although most of the stuff we drink comes out of vats somewhere in California. The dry outsells the sweet by about 3 to 1.

WHISKEY—An alcoholic distillate of the fermented

mash of some kind of grain. Among the more popular varieties:

American whiskies:

—Rye: made from malted rye or barley.

—Bourbon: originally made from corn, but now mostly from wheat, barley or rye. It gets its flavor from being aged in charred barrels.

—Corn: made from corn, and by the same process as moonshiner's "white lightning," it doesn't have to be aged in barrels like bourbon.

Canadian whiskey: chiefly made of wheat and rye, it is always aged at least two years, always a straight (I'll explain this later) and usually a blend (I'll get to that, too).

Scotch: made in Scotland, at least three years old, and usually a blend of malt and grain whiskies.

Irish whiskey: made from malted barley and rye, is usually a straight, and must, by law, be a minimum of five years old.

About blends, straights and bonds:

The government has strict rules about what goes into different kinds of U.S. whiskies, and it says on the label what they are:

—A blend: has to have at least 20% 100 proof straight whiskey; the rest can be either other kinds of whiskey or neutral spirits. So it can be only 20% real whiskey, and the rest water, grain alcohol, colorings and flavorings.

—A straight: whiskey of from 80 to 110 proof, aged not less than two years in new, charred-oak barrels. (You can also get a blend of straight whiskies, as in Canadian and Scotch types, without neutral spirits.)

—A bond is a straight bottled under government supervision, and must be 100 proof and at least four years old.

So a bond is the best straight, which means it is all

whiskey. Some blends which aren't made of 100% straight whiskey may be quite tasty—the neutral spirits, some feel, cut the bourbon flavor and make for a lighter, milder taste. It can be a nice drink, but, for my money, it isn't whiskey.

The Ultimate Weapon

or

An Itsy, Bitsy, Teeny, Weeny Extra Special Dry Martini

There are those who'll tell you the name martini comes from Martini and Rossi, the Italian vermouth makers. But I prefer the San Francisco story:

Before bridges spanned the bay, a ferry ran across to the Oakland side, and to the town of Martinez. This one fellow used to stop in at the Ferry Building bar and order his favorite drink: gin and vermouth, chilled and strained into a big wine glass. "Quick!" he'd say. "I gotta get to Martinez."

Other customers tried it and liked it. "Just time for a Martinez," they'd say, and the drink became known as a Martinez cocktail. Somewhere along the line singular became martini and plural martinis.

Oldtime recipes called for making the original Martinez cocktail from a liqueur glass of gin and a wine glass of vermouth. They were on the right track, but they had their ingredients reversed. It was known before the first World War as a mixture of two parts gin to one of vermouth. In "A Farewell to Arms," set in WWI, Hemingway had the hero say: "I had a couple of martinis. I had never tasted anything so cool and clean. They made me feel civilized. I had had too much red wine, bad coffee and grappa."

To make a man feel civilized it must've been drier than 2-to-1. Martinis kept getting drier. By World War II the standard recipe was 4-to-1. Later it got to 5-to-1, 6-to-1 and 15-to-1. After that came the sort of recipes which, when used, make it advisable for you to collect everyone's car keys:

—Pour vermouth over the ice, pour it out, and add the gin, which mixes with the vermouth still in the ice. In Korea my flying mates referred to this as a McTini, but I must admit in all modesty I didn't invent it.

—Spray vermouth (aerosol cans are available) over the top of a glass filled with chilled gin.

—Let the vermouth bottle sit nearby, but don't open it. Chill the gin and drink it straight.

Purists (Bill and I among them) insist that vermouth is an important, if minority, constituent of the modern martini. How do I make mine? I like to use a silver mixer—it gets cold quicker. But first I introduce the ingredients together when they're warm, so they can get to know each other better. First the gin, then the vermouth, at about 5-to-1. (I've gotten more conservative since Korea.) Then I shock them with more ice than you'd really think is necessary. North of the equator you stir counterclockwise.

However it's made, it's still the most popular cocktail in America and the world. Did you know there was a reference to it in Kipling? One of my favorites. In 1892 he wrote about it in a poem about the Fuzzy Wuzzy, the bushy-haired native in the Sudan who once "broke the British square." Remember those old movies where the general, played by C. Aubrey Smith, lined his men up in a hollow square? Wrote Kipling:

"We sloshed you with Martinis, an' it wasn't 'ardly fair."

'Ardly fair my C. Aubrey! It was inhuman! Can you picture the redcoats lined up in their pith helmets, pitchers

163

at the ready, waiting for the Fuzzy Wuzzies to charge up, cold sober, and get it? It was the ultimate weapon, I decided. The effect, I thought, must've been staggering.

Later I was disappointed to learn that the Martini was a rifle. I guess the burdens of imperialism didn't include bartending.

Let me close this section with my favorite Personal Experience. You know, My Most Unforgettable Martini sort of thing:

One Sunday I was home alone about 4:30, and I decided it was time for a martini. Fortunately there were a couple of glasses chilled from the night before, and my silver pitcher was still in the refrigerator, filled with ice. I began to make a martini, and as I did so I began to have a feeling that there was something very special about this martini. The color was perfect—a white but lightly amber tint. And very, very cold.

As I poured the martini, oddly enough there was enough in the pitcher to fill the second glass, too. So I poured it and set them both before me. I took a sip, and I knew instantly that this was the greatest martini I had ever made. When I'd taken my second sip, I was sure it was not only my greatest martini, but the greatest martini that had ever been mixed in the whole world.

And as I stood there all alone in the kitchen, sipping my martini, a hand came down from heaven—and took the other martini.

The Curse of the
Drinking Man
or
The Care, Treatment
and Cause of The
American Hangover

The first hangover occurred the morning after the invention of history's first more than merely flavorsome beverage. It's still with us, my friends tell me. (As a man of moderation, and thus not susceptible to this problem, I've had to find out about it from my friends, poor devils.) I know this one guy who is enraged about the government spending all those millions to send men to the moon when it still hasn't done anything about mornings after here on earth. The truth is, although there are a few hundred thousand theories on what to do about the hangover, none seems to work much better than just waiting for survival to set in. But most people feel waiting isn't enough; you've got to do something.

I read where a doctor at the Rutgers Center for Alcoholic Studies (who says our academic institutions lack relevance?) explained that there's not much you can do about a hangover, because of what too much alcohol does to you: it discombobulates the entire central nervous system. It causes changes in the distribution of water in the brain and body (the Sahara tongue syndrome), upsets the salt and sugar balance in your system (bland blood is unhappy blood) and clogs your stomach with hydrochloric acid (which makes your stomach feel like it's full of hydrochloric acid).

The Rutgers researchers say that the best thing to do is roll over and go back to sleep. That's great for you researchers, who have to get that report finished by 1975. But what about a guy who has to be at work at 9:00?

First, there are steps to take the night before. One is abstinence, which is for another book—not this one. The next is moderation. Fine, but what if you fall among evil companions? There are some things you can still do; drink lots of water before you go to bed, to fight dehydration; take some salt pills, to fight desalinization; take an antacid (pills, powders, soothing medicines) to fight all that acid. (The acid is part of your normal digestive juices, whose flow is stimulated by alcohol.)

The best precaution, according to the Rutgers findings, would be to allow yourself a day and a half to sleep. They say that it takes 12 to 36 hours for the body to get back to normal after a really big night. So, when you go to bed Saturday night, plan to sleep until about noon Monday. It's a cinch. No hangover.

But some people can't wait that long.

What can be done in less than 12 hours? Let's take a look at the folklore of hangover cures, and see what has worked, sometime, for some people.

Rise and Shine With:

—Beef bouillon: It restores lost potassium and helps overcome fatigue.

—Orange or cranberry juice: the sucrose will replace lost glycogen, relieving disorientation.

—Vitamins: they help ease jangled nerves and ease out upsets in your system. Especially recommended: Vitamin B1.

—Aspirin: With an upset stomach, try the buffered kind.

167

—Take a powder: those bubbling powders and tablets have aspirin in them, and they help get your stomach back to normal. That's where the battle began, you know.

—Steam baths: to soak out the evil residues.

—Cold showers: they feel so good when you stop.

—Jogging: some swear it helps. Like a steam bath, perhaps.

—Oxygen: I knew a hospital intern once who insisted pure oxygen—which he probably stole from someone who really needed it—clears the brain.

I've seen people so badly stricken they've tried all of those almost simultaneously (some claim it helps to keep busy). Ever try jogging in an oxygen mask? Then there are those who'll take these measures, plus one more:

Hair of the Dog

The old saying about partaking of the hair of the dog that bit you probably stems from this song, author unknown, dating back to at least 1650:

But be sure overnight,
If this dog do you bite,
You may take it henceforth for a warning;
Soon as out of your bed,
To settle your head,
Take a hair of his tail in the morning.

There's some validity to this, medically—a recovery drink raises the level of your blood sugar quickly, and you do feel better. (Pure cranberry juice would do this, too, but somehow it isn't quite the same.)

One bite-back version holds that you should open a can of beer before you go to bed, and, in the morning, drink it—flat and warm—as fast as you can.

Another is to take a couple of shots of what you were drinking the night before. If you were drinking Scotch, pour down some Scotch. But what happens to people who got stoned, Bacchus forbid, on something like Grasshoppers? Or Pousse Cafes? Aargh!

Remember how Jeeves, P.G. Wodehouse's perfect butler, first got his job with Bertie Wooster? He arrived from the employment agency the morning Bertie was suffering from the aftermath of a big evening at the Drones Club. Jeeves took one look and immediately repaired to the kitchen, returning with a mixture Bertie quickly downed. After he bounced off a couple of walls and got his eyes back in their sockets, he and the drink settled down, the sun suddenly came out, the birds began singing, and survival became not only possible, but desirable. "Jeeves," said Bertie, "You're engaged."

What was in Jeeves' concoction? Raw eggs, tomato juice, Worcestershire sauce, red pepper and vodka.

My favorite cure for a hangover comes from a Ninevite (Mesopotamia) tablet around 3,000 B.C. It also contains, incidentally, the earliest clinical description of intoxication on record.

"If a man has taken strong wine, his head is affected

and he forgets his words and his speech becomes confused, his mind wanders and his eyes have a set expression; to cure him—licorice, beans, oleander (and eight other unidentified substances) to be compounded with oil and wine before sunset, and in the morning before sunrise . . . let him take it *before anyone has kissed him* (italics mine) and he will recover."

The Loaded Sobriety
Test or
How To Send Them
Home Filled with
Confidence
(Among Other Things)

Charge your glasses one more time, ladies and gentlemen. The party's almost over.

But first, it's time for a sobriety test. Uncle Ed's loaded sobriety test.

Walking a line? Forget it. My sobriety test is harder than that. It could flunk the steering committee of the Prohibition Party. For openers, let's see if our drinking friends can do these:

—Ask the soberest guy there to place his head against the wall, with his feet about three feet from it. Then tell him to regain his upright position without using his hands.

(Guess what . . . It's impossible.)

—Stand someone against a wall with his heels together. Place a dollar bill on the floor right in front of him (or his driver's license, if the giddy fool thinks he's going to drive home). Have him pick up the object with his heels against the wall without bending his knees.

(It's impossible. He'll fall forward before he comes close to it.)

—Ask the subject to stand sideways against a wall so that the entire side of his right shoe is against the wall. Ask him to lift his left foot.

(Can't be done. He'll lose his balance and start to fall sideways.)

—Demonstrate this one yourself, first, to set your victim up for it: Wet a dime or a quarter and press it against your forehead; then show how you can make it fall off by waggling your eyebrows. Then do the same with the taker of the test. Except, when you put the quarter on his forehead, secretly take the coin away.

(He *thinks* he's flunking this one, because nothing falls off his forehead. The harder he tries the wilder his facial contortions become. As long as his forehead is damp, he'll think something is still there. Flunk him—by pretending to remove a quarter palmed in your hand—before he realizes there's nothing there.)

One more test!

My friend, Al, had to move off South Shadyside Street, because he was always incriminating himself when a cop asked him where he was going after he left a bar. His address was a tongue twister! Most sobriety tests don't include such things. But mine does.

Ask your friends to say these five times before you'll let them drive home:

Smith's fish sauce shop seldom sells shell fish
Rubber buggy bumper
Abdominally abominable
Phenomenally pornographic phonograph
Mix Miss Mix
What a shame such shapely sashes show such shabby stilted stitches
Blue blood bad blood

—Have we let in someone who's almost a teetotaler? Or, even worse, a total teetotaler—you, a teetotalitarian? Let him try this:

Put his forefinger on the floor, and, leaning over, holding it there, have him make five complete turns.

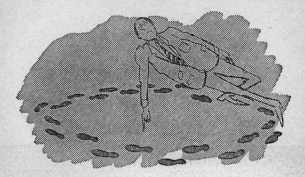

(It sounds easy. But believe me, by the fifth time around, he'll have caught up with the rest of the gathering.)

Drinking for Profit

or

They Said It Couldn't Be Done And It Can't

Here's an idea: why not start a saloon in your own home? Since you're going to be the only customer, you won't need a license. Buy a gallon of whiskey (costing about $28) and set it up on your home bar. Do all your drinking at home, and let your wife handle the money. Pay her $1 for every drink. There are 128 1-ounce drinks in a gallon. If you buy six a day, in 21 days you'll have emptied the jug—and your wife will be able to buy another gallon, and put $100 profit into the bank.

At the end of the year she'll have $1,700 to bank. If

she invests it at a decent rate of interest, at the end of ten years she'll have more than $22,500 socked away. And, if something happens to you—after some 170 gallons of home booze—she'll be able to bury you respectfully and, as a rich widow, she'll be able to attract and marry a decent man and forget she ever knew you.

Gentlemen,
Charge Your Glasses!

In the past, when the military enjoyed more glorious days, the Formal Mess was an all-military affair where officers gathered in formal uniform and presented a series of toasts. I attended one once at the Union League in Philadelphia when the First Philadelphia Corps was being reunited with the Black Watch Corps from Canada. In front of each man was a large bottle of wine and a glass. Someone stood up and said: "I propose a toast to the Queen of England. Gentlemen, charge your glasses!" Everyone stood up, filled his glass, raised it high, and finished the wine. Then, everyone sat down. Another officer stood up and said: "I propose a toast to the Prince of Wales. Gentlemen, charge your glasses!" The procedure was repeated. It went on through the hierarchy of England, Canada and the United States. By the time they got to the U.S. Chief of Staff the wine was gone. And so was the assemblage.

Surely It Can't Be
Closing Time!

. . . Did you see Bill put that two dollar alarm clock prominently on the cash register? Did you ever notice you can never find a clock in a bar until it's time to close, and then it's 10 minutes fast?

But it's been a great evening. I think we've covered the Drinking Movement in America, and we've had a little fun along the way. Didn't I tell you this was a great little place to waste some time waiting for your wife? I used to . . .

MY WIFE!

I just remembered! Wasn't I supposed to call her and tell her where to meet me?

Well, it's too late now. Worse than that, it's 10 minutes past too late. But she'll understand. It's happened before. I'll tell her I was just waiting for the ice to melt.

DON'T STOP THE CARNIVAL

HERMAN WOUK

95022 / 95¢

is clock-racingly readable, with a comic line that
moves as fast as a Marx Brothers movie..."
—*The New York Times*

If your bookseller does not have this title, you may
order it by sending retail price, plus 15¢ for mailing
and handling to: MAIL SERVICE DEPARTMENT,
POCKET BOOKS, A Division of Simon & Schuster,
Inc., 1 West 39th St., New York, N.Y. 10018. Not
responsible for orders containing cash. Please send
check or money order.

PUBLISHED BY
POCKET BOOKS
(A 4/9)

2,000 INSULTS FOR ALL OCCASIONS . . 55056/60¢
2,000 MORE INSULTS . . . . 55057/60¢
THE BEST OF SICK JOKES . . . . 55055/60¢

G 4/9

⚓ PUBLISHED BY
POCKET BOOKS

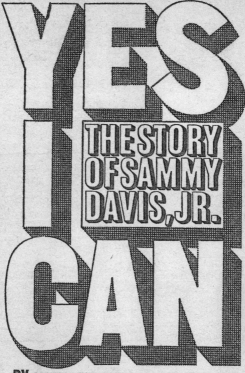

YES I CAN

THE STORY OF SAMMY DAVIS, JR.

BY SAMMY DAVIS, JR. AND JANE AND BURT BOYAR

95034/95¢

If your bookseller does not have this title, you may
order it by sending retail price, plus 15¢ for mailing
and handling to: MAIL SERVICE DEPARTMENT,
POCKET BOOKS, A Division of Simon & Schuster,
Inc., 1 West 39th St., New York, N.Y. 10018. Not
responsible for orders containing cash. Please send
check or money order.

PUBLISHED BY
POCKET BOOKS

(G 1/9)